BLUE RIBBON
VEGETABLE GARDENING

IOWA
STATE
FAIR

IowaStateFair

DES MOINES

FIRST
PLACE

★BLUE★
RIBBON
VEGETABLE
GARDENING

THE SECRETS TO GROWING THE BIGGEST AND BEST PRIZEWINNING PRODUCE ★ JODI TORPEY

635
Tor

The mission of Storey Publishing is to serve our customers by
publishing practical information that encourages
personal independence in harmony with the environment.

EDITED BY Carleen Madigan and Elizabeth P. Stell
ART DIRECTION BY Carolyn Eckert
COVER DESIGN BY Jeff Canham and Carolyn Eckert
BOOK DESIGN BY Kelley Galbreath
INDEXED BY Christine R. Lindemer, Boston Road Communications

COVER PHOTOGRAPHY BY © Ryan Donnell, except author's photograph by © John Pendleton
Interior photography credits appear on page 215.

Storey Publishing
210 MASS MoCA Way
North Adams, MA 01247
www.storey.com

Printed in China by R.R. Donnelley
10 9 8 7 6 5 4 3 2 1

Library of Congress Cataloging-in-Publication Data

Torpey, Jodi B., 1953- author.
  Blue ribbon vegetable gardening / by Jodi Torpey.
    pages cm
  Includes bibliographical references.
  ISBN 978-1-61212-394-3 (pbk. : alk. paper)
  ISBN 978-1-61212-395-0 (ebook) 1. Vegetable
  gardening. 2. Vegetable gardening—Competitions.
  I. Title.
SB321.T67 2015
635—dc23
                                    2015014315

WINNER
'Red Cloud' beets
Don Francois

WINNER
'Beefsteak' tomato
Joyce Fisher

WINNER
'Sweet Banana' pepper
Daniel Cretors

WINNER
'Black Beauty'
eggplant
Robert Morris

WINNER
'Dragon Tongue'
beans
Larry Dau

IowaStateFair

WINNER
'Bangkok'
hot pepper
Valerie Singer

WINNER
'Yellow Scorpion'
hot pepper
Jillian Romine

WINNER
Savoy cabbage
Larry Dau

IOWA
STATE
FAIR

DES MOINES

VERALL
INNER
& HORT
ROPS

WINNER
'Palace King'
cucumber
Larry Dau

WINNER
'Carnival' squash
Larry Dau

CONTENTS

IOWA STATE FAIR
DES MOINES
FIRST PLACE
AG & HORT CROPS

IOWA STATE FAIR
DES MOINES
FIRST PLACE

IOWA STATE FAIR
DES MOINES
FIRST

IOWA STATE FAIR

AGRICULTURE BUILDING

2014 Iowa State Fair
VEGETABLE CROPS
130 207
Division   Class   PLACING
Variety Big Boy

DIVISION   CLASS
130   207

PLACING   PREMIUM

★ PREFACE ★

ONE OF THE HIGHLIGHTS OF SUMMER for this city kid was an annual trip to the Colorado State Fair. While my friends spent their time (and money) at the midway, I was content to wander through the animal barns. I daydreamed about owning a lop-eared bunny, taking care of a pet chicken, and raising a Shetland pony in my suburban backyard. I also spent a lot of time in the Creative Arts building admiring the blue ribbons attached to charming quilts, hand-painted china, and jars of soldier-straight green beans.

I really wanted to win one of those beautiful blue rosettes, but I didn't have the patience for quilting, and I knew I could never learn to paint a perfect rose. However I did know a little something about vegetables.

The first time I won a blue ribbon for some of my homegrown veggies, I had an unexpected emotional response. I still recall the precontest butterflies, hoping that one of my entries might catch the judges' attention — and the resulting delight when my sweet basil, hot peppers, and cherry tomatoes all gained a top prize. I remember that day like it was yesterday.

That's because it was. After growing vegetable gardens for more than 30 years, I entered my first horticulture competition in 2012. Thanks to good gardening weather, I was able to take three entries to a county fair. Thanks to beginner's luck, I came home with three satin blue ribbons. My exuberance caused one of the fair clerks to say, "Next year you can enter more."

That's what I'm still afraid of. I've heard about home gardeners entering a vegetable competition one year "just for the fun it" and then becoming obsessed with growing bigger and better the following year. An enjoyable hobby can become a year-round preoccupation to unlock gardening's secrets and fine-tune every part of the growing process. As one gardener said after his initial success, "I haven't had a holiday since."

But if you're a gardener whose feet are firmly planted on the ground, you'll find that growing vegetables for competition injects new joy into your gardening efforts. You'll also join a long line of farmers and gardeners who began exhibiting at agricultural shows almost as soon as the first events took root.

Competitive gardening is similar to other competitive sports. Medals, ribbons, and prize money are nice, but gardeners enter their vegetables in contests for the pleasure of seeing how their skill stacks up against the competition. They also get validation for the personal accomplishment of growing something wonderful from a handful of seeds.

This book is for gardeners of all skill levels who want the competitive challenge of growing prizewinning produce. It includes everything you need to know about the horticulture competition process, from locating contests and studying the rules to tips for thinking like a judge.

I wrote this book for another type of gardener, too — for growers who'd simply like to find ways to improve their vegetable gardening efforts. The tips in this guide are equally useful for those who'd like to harvest high-quality produce for eating instead of competing.

The first chapter surveys the history of this sport. Reading about gardening in the old days gives you a window into what interested gardeners most at that time. Learning how agricultural exhibitions evolved in England, and how American horticulturists worked to catch up, will connect you with the wonderful tradition of entering vegetable contests.

Chapter 2 gives you the nitty-gritty details of how to enter a vegetable competition. It covers the basics of growing for competition, how to prepare your produce for the contest, and helpful hints on what judges are looking for in prizewinners.

The remaining chapters tell you how to grow champion produce. Each covers one of the top 10 fruits and vegetables entered in contests today. I chose these because they're some of the most popular edibles gardeners grow. Plus they can be planted just about anywhere, from large farm gardens to small urban plots and balcony and patio containers or wherever an industrious gardener can find a sunny spot.

I hope you'll enjoy the historical quotes, anecdotes, and gardening trivia planted throughout each chapter. It's easy to take for granted our garden-grown vegetables, but each traveled its own road to get to our tables and all deserve to be celebrated. As Evelyne Bloch-Dano wrote in *Vegetables: A Biography*, "Because vegetables connect us to the earth . . . they occupy a very specific place in the history of food, as well as in our imaginations, our myths, our customs, our family heritages."

While researching and writing this book, I visited pumpkin patches of astonishing proportions, got lost among the pages of old gardening books, watched giant vegetable weigh-offs, and competed at state and county fairs. I even won a few blue ribbons in the process.

I can't promise you'll gain fame or fortune by entering your homegrown vegetables in a contest, even if you follow every strategy. What I can promise is that you'll have a bit of fun, meet some interesting folks, and gain a new appreciation for the traditions of our country's rich agricultural heritage. If you need a simple mantra to encourage you to plant a prizewinning garden, remember this: *Seeds want to sprout; plants want to grow.*

CHAPTER 1

THE COMPETITIVE LEGACY

YOU KNOW YOU GROW GREAT TOMATOES. YOUR FAMILY KNOWS you grow great tomatoes. Heck, even your neighbors can't wait to get their hands on your garden-grown goodies. So why not take your best vegetables to the fair for some official accolades? Like the fair's other competitive events, a vegetable competition is a challenging opportunity to walk away with ribbons and some prize money. If you happen to have a natural competitive spirit, the bragging rights alone may be the best reward of all.

IT'S AS MUCH FUN AS A FERRIS wheel to enter a vegetable contest and be part of the excitement of a fair. In the days leading up to a contest you have to balance nervous anticipation with the daily gardening routine. Gardening for competition requires monitoring progress, dealing with wild weather, making adjustments, and trying to outsmart Mother Nature. Then, finally, comes the exhilaration of the actual event.

Winning ribbons for picture-perfect produce is a splendid reward for a season of working in the garden, but you can win prizes for oddball vegetables, too. One time I was tickled to take home the top prize for funniest mutation in the novelty vegetable class. Two of my tomatoes had grown together to form a perfectly round miniature derriére. I titled my winning entry How I Got a Little Behind in My Gardening.

That oddball tomato is just one example of what you might get from your garden. The tomato that seems to be winking owes its funny form to catfacing caused by weather that's too cold while blossoms were forming. The carrot that looks like it's wearing pants grew in rocky soil that caused the root to split in two. The cucumber with the long neck and small head grew into its strange shape because of poor pollination or inconsistent watering. So don't worry if your vegetables aren't picture-perfect. You can still have lots of fun, especially with a good sense of humor.

HORSE RACING AND HORTICULTURE

Since medieval times, fairs have been held to attract crowds. Some groups gathered together for religious purposes, others for trade and commerce, and many had educational aspirations. No matter the reason, all fairs eventually evolved into social and shopping occasions that included entertainment. Fairs haven't changed much in all these years.

As agricultural exhibitions grew in America, organizers added attractions to boost attendance. Horse racing became popular (and money-making) entertainment at fairs, despite strong opposition from some quarters. The 1881 book *How to Manage Agricultural Fairs*

HIGH-CLASS VEGETABLES

WHILE SEARCHING THROUGH antiquated gardening publications for clues to the origins of vegetable competitions in America, I came across a book called *The English Vegetable Garden*. The editors of *Country Life Limited*, an esteemed British weekly magazine, published this classic guide in 1909, when fine gardening was a popular pastime.

Sandwiched between "Vegetables Neglected in English Gardens" and "Salads" is the chapter "Vegetables for Exhibition." This chapter details how gardeners can grow and exhibit quality vegetables. "No branch of gardening deserves more encouragement than the culture of high-class vegetables," the authors wrote. "Good vegetables are the necessities of life, and it is profitable and pleasurable to grow them to perfection."

The emphasis on growing "high-class" vegetables is significant. In all previous years, judges rated vegetables only by size and weight. Color, uniformity, and other standards of perfection weren't considered essential to selecting the winners.

/Horticulture: Novelty, Funniest/Mutation / Shape

"...s" or "How I Got a Little Behind in My Gardening" is a
...heirloom tomato variety called 'Glacier' (*Lycopersicon*

...to-leaf foliage and is known for setting loads of small,
... tomatoes. Apparently this plant was caught sitting
...lob.

Denver County Fair!

1st PLACE

2012

Even weirdly shaped vegetables and funny fruits — like my 'Glacier' tomatoes — can win blue ribbons when entered in the novelty vegetable category at the county fair.

WHY so BLUE?

HAVE YOU EVER WONDERED why first-place ribbons are usually the color blue? The use of blue to recognize high honors dates to England around 1344. That's when King Edward III founded the Order of the Garter, one of the most distinguished military honors of knighthood. The Order included 25 knights who wore uniforms of blue cloth. Changes made to their garb over the years included the addition of a gold medallion, representing St. George and the dragon, that's worn suspended from a blue ribbon.

were also firework displays, band concerts, sideshows, and vendors selling trinkets, food, drinks, and sweets.

Despite all the added attractions, every fair's purpose was to showcase improvements in farming and to award prizes to the best specimens of crops, fruits, and vegetables. The agricultural competitions converged with two other important developments: an increased demand for better produce in the marketplace, and plant breeders' work to improve the quality, productivity, and appearance of many vegetables.

BREEDING LEADS ᴛᴏ COMPETING

Today's gardeners would have a difficult time identifying the vegetables our ancestors ate. Wild tomatoes looked like yellow berries growing on bushes, and carrots were nothing more than white, rangy roots. It took years for vegetables to grow into the ones we recognize today. Gardeners owe a debt of thanks to those first farmers who dug tubers from the earth to feed their families and then kept the tastiest to transplant and grow again.

Compared to what gardeners plant today, early farms and gardens didn't offer much vegetable diversity. If we were transported back in time and could peek into a medieval English garden, we might see beans, cabbages, onions, leeks, lettuce, and peas. Mercifully, the world of vegetables mushroomed in the 1400s when intrepid explorers transported plants and agricultural products from one part of the globe to another. That's how corn (maize), potatoes, and beans from the Americas found their way into European dining rooms.

Agriculture took a giant leap forward in 1700s England when "gentlemen farmers" began to experiment with new concepts in tillage, cultivation, seed selection, and crop rotation. Informal sharing of ideas, inventions, and agricultural improvements grew into formal

specifies the buildings needed on a fairground, including the ring: "Without here discussing the question of racing and its moral bearings, we say that it is usual to lay out a ring of some character, to exercise and speed horses upon."

It didn't take long for other amusements to work their way into fairs. Today's traveling carnivals started in small tents that featured games of chance and numerous "fakirs" to entertain (if not fleece) the attendants. There

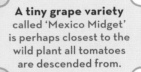

A tiny grape variety called 'Mexico Midget' is perhaps closest to the wild plant all tomatoes are descended from.

membership societies to encourage advances in farming. The Society of Improvers in the Knowledge of Agriculture was one of the earliest groups, started in 1723. The members of these societies met regularly for education and socializing. The larger groups held agricultural shows and awarded premiums for successful experiments, whether for cultivating the largest amount of land for growing early potatoes or for finding a cure for sheep rot.

FLOWER FÊTES
ᶦᴺ BRITAIN

Agricultural and horticultural societies of all sizes flourished during the late 1700s, and members were inspired to share their successes. Some of the largest flower and vegetable shows held in the United Kingdom today were started by these societies two hundred years ago.

Britain's venerable Royal Horticultural Society (RHS) opened its doors in 1804. By about 1818, every kind of fruit and vegetable appeared

"in its season" at exhibitions held during the society's meetings. The society's well-respected flower shows that flourish today began in the late 1820s as society floral fairs held at the Duke of Devonshire's estate. There was so much interest in the exhibitions that British horticultural newspapers reported the results.

As these flower and vegetable shows became more popular, they evolved into bigger events. A classic example is the St. Ives Flower and Produce Show in Cambridgeshire, England. The first contest of the Cottagers' Horticultural Society, staged on July 22, 1876, included 20 classes of vegetables and 11 classes of fruit.

Twelve years later, the St. Ives Flower Show had become an important fixture in the county and "the principal floricultural and horticultural exhibition in the shire." *The Hunts Guardian & East Midland Spectator* newspaper called it "a brilliant success." That show added extravagant elements like decorations of flags, fairy lamps, and Chinese lanterns. A flying trapeze took up a large part of the tennis ground, and the

GREAT TEXAS STATE FAIR AND DALLAS EXPOSITION

AT

DALLAS, TEXAS

* * * THE NINTH ANNUAL ENTERTAINMENT AT DALLAS * * *

OPENS OCT. 20th, CLOSES NOV. 4th

16 DAYS. LARGER, GRANDER AND MORE MAGNIFICENT THAN EVER.

PREMIUMS AND PURSES, $75,000.00

* ATTRACTIONS OF UNUSUAL EXCELLENCE *
SELECTED WITH GREAT CARE AND EXPENSE.

PROF. LIBERATTI
With his celebrated and world-renowned MILITARY BAND AND CONCERT COMPANY
will give performances daily

NUMEROUS OUT-DOOR ATTRACTIONS DAILY AND NIGHTLY

NEW BUILDINGS
ERECTED FOR THE ACCOMMODATION OF ALL KINDS OF LIVE STOCK.

EXPOSITION AND MACHINERY HALLS
Remodeled, offering a special inducement to exhibitors to make fine displays.

THIRTEEN DAYS RACING
Five Races Each Day. Two Tracks, one for Runners, and one for Trotters and Pacers.

A GRAND AGRICULTURAL AND HORTICULTURAL EXHIBIT!

LOW RATES ON ALL RAILROADS!

CATALOGUES, PREMIUM LISTS, RACE PROGRAMMES, CIRCULARS, ETC., MAILED ON APPLICATION.

A. SANGER, ... President.   C. A. COUR, ... Secretary.

THE UNITED STATES PT'G. CO. RUSSELL & MORGAN, FACTORIES, CIN, O.

"Celebrated Yokohama Troupe" entertained the crowd with juggling and balancing acts. The Rushden Temperance Silver Prize Band performed twice in one day.

Around this time, at the end of the nineteenth century, the RHS adopted a set of formal rules for judging the quality of the specimens on exhibition. No longer were vegetables judged on size alone, but also on their general appearance and taste.

AGRICULTURAL EXHIBITIONS IN EARLY AMERICA

Today's county and state fairs are direct descendants of the agricultural shows and sales that began in early America as regular market days and fairs. As early as 1686 the first session of the New Jersey Assembly set aside every Wednesday as market day and the first Tuesdays in May and October for fairs, each lasting three days. Those early fairs included horse races, booths with streamers, and "a heterogeneous collection of articles for sale."

In the largely rural, agrarian society of early America, people began to form agricultural groups, similar to the societies organized by the gentlemen farmers in England. Distinguished members of the Philadelphia Society for Promoting Agriculture included George Washington and Benjamin Franklin. Other societies followed with the goal of improving commerce, stimulating trade, and expanding the economy in a country that was still young and working toward self-sufficiency.

The annual sheepshearing events George Washington Parke Custis held on his Arlington, Virginia, estate were modeled after similar events in England. Watching sheep being sheared doesn't sound like a reason to get all gussied up today, but in the early 1800s social occasions like these attracted a highbrow crowd.

CORN CLUBS FOR BOYS

CORN-GROWING CONTESTS

helped encourage a new generation of farmers near the turn of the twentieth century. The president of a county farmers' institute in Illinois, Will B. Otwell, organized these contests to encourage boys to plant corn in spring, compete to grow the largest yield, and exhibit that fall. Hundreds of boys signed on for free high-quality corn seeds and the chance to win a $1 premium. These contests eventually grew into what were called boys' corn clubs. The success of these clubs led to organizing tomato canning clubs for girls around 1910. These clubs were the forerunners of the well-known international network of youth development organizations we recognize today: 4-H.

America's gentlemen farmers benefited from these livestock events, but ordinary farmers were too busy farming to take part. Elkanah Watson, a successful farmer and businessman, changed that in 1807 when he displayed two of his Merino sheep to the general public in Pittsfield, Massachusetts. Showing off two sheep might not seem like a momentous occasion, but that event helped Watson earn his title as "father of the agricultural fair." His Berkshire Agricultural Society started annual fairs and competitions that grew in the number of participants, contests, and prizes. He also added parades, plowing matches, and grand agricultural balls — many of the same elements that are part of county and state fairs today.

It was around 1840 that agricultural societies came into their own as a way to boost the American economy. During the next 20 years, almost a thousand societies sprang up as state or county organizations, all with the primary purpose of holding annual fairs.

These exhibitions and fairs were highly anticipated social events. Farmers and their families visited fairs to study new methods for raising livestock; watch demonstrations of farming equipment; learn about developments in planting, tilling, and harvesting; see the latest in the domestic arts; and compete for the "agricultural ideal" in crop and horticultural contests.

The resurgence of interest in fairs between 1850 and 1870 was so great that the founder of the Cooperative Extension Service at Land Grant Universities, Kenyon L. Butterfield, referred to those two decades as "the golden age of the agricultural fair."

DEVELOPING A COMPETITIVE EDGE

Today's vegetable contests wouldn't be as interesting if it weren't for the work of plant breeders starting in the mid-1800s. American agriculturists and horticulturists were especially interested in applying Gregor Mendel's principles for using genetics to improve crops.

It wasn't long after Mendel published the results of his experiments with pea plants that Luther Burbank had his first important horticultural discovery. In 1873, the "gardener to the world" found a rare potato seed ball that became the famed 'Russet Burbank' potato, the same beautiful Idaho baking potato grown today. Burbank conducted his plant breeding experiments in California and introduced more than eight hundred new varieties of plants including hundreds of ornamental flowers and more than two hundred varieties of fruits, vegetables, nuts, and grains.

MORE THAN A CENTURY IN THE MAKING

MOST COUNTY FAIRS have a long history, and many celebrated their 100th anniversary years ago. But Denver, Colorado, didn't get its fair until 2011. Back in 1863, Denver started planning for a fair on a 40-acre site east of the city, but budget problems and the ongoing Civil War caused delays. Almost 150 years passed between the idea of a county fair and the day the fair opened its doors. It took a pair of enterprising entrepreneurs to revive the county fair and give it an urban twist. By then, the original fairground site had become Denver's City Park.

Extensive experimental work in plant breeding began in earnest at the turn of the twentieth century. Each year seed and plant companies promoted their new, improved varieties that were said to be more disease resistant, more productive, and better tasting. But the average farmer or gardener had no way to know if the seeds lived up to their hype.

ALL-AMERICA SELECTIONS

Horticulturist W. Ray Hastings of Harrisburg, Pennsylvania, recognized the need for a network of independent trial gardens for testing new flowers and vegetables. He started All-America Selections (AAS) in 1932 to help gardeners find reliable varieties that lived up to their claims of being "new and improved."

If it weren't for the work of Mendel and Burbank (who found and named the 'Russet Burbank' potato), we wouldn't have such a vast number of vegetable varieties to enter in competitions.

As president of the Southern Seedsmen's Association, Hastings was able to launch the program one year and release results the next.

AAS announced 19 new varieties of flowers and vegetables in 1933, and the organization has named new crops of winners every year since. The sugar snap pea, introduced as a completely new vegetable in 1979, is one of the organization's success stories. Prior to this introduction, there were only two kinds of peas: the English pea and the snow pea, but the sugar snap pea combined the best qualities of the two. AAS continues as an independent testing organization, coordinating the trialing process in test gardens across the country and recommending winners every year.

While new and improved vegetables are introduced to gardeners year after year, vegetable competitions haven't changed much from those early agricultural contests. Farmers and gardeners work all season to grow a good crop of fruits and vegetables to take to a fair, judges make their selections, and the best specimens receive recognition.

The authors of *The English Vegetable Garden* understood this process, too. "Those who are thinking and hoping to excel in the production of high-class vegetables must remember that much work and forethought are needful," they wrote. "Those who persevere are the ones to succeed. Success is not a matter of mere luck as some imagine."

CHAPTER 2

WHY NOT
GIVE IT A GO?

VEGETABLES DON'T DO WELL WHEN THEY HAVE TO COMPETE
with other plants, but the same can't be said about the gardeners who grow them. For some growers, a competitive nature is simply hardwired into their green thumbs. These gardeners are eager to place a friendly gardening bet long before the first seeds are planted and then yak about their garden all season long.

GOOD-NATURED GARDENING banter probably started as soon as the first vegetable gardens were planted. Even Thomas Jefferson had a gentleman's bet to see which neighbor could harvest the first edible English pea each year. Friendly wagers are the norm, but gardening can turn serious when the stakes are high. I've read about pumpkin sabotage right before a weigh-off and vandals using knives, axes, or shovels to attack a crop of giant leeks before an exhibition.

Marty Schnicker and his giant kohlrabi

IN THE YEARS between 1926 and 1930, the total of the prizes awarded at the Iowa State Fair grew from $23,635 to $124,256. There were more entries in the competitions, and fair organizers also started awarding prize money to more than just the highest ranked winners in each contest. More prize money meant better quality agricultural products, too.

Competition exists in all horticultural pursuits. The extremely passionate rose exhibitors called roseaholics grow roses for the sole purpose of exhibiting them and collecting crystal trophies. Some impassioned rose gardeners have lost marriages to the hobby because it's so consuming. Unlike these roseaholics described by Aurelia Scott in her book *Otherwise Normal People*, vegetable gardeners would probably plant a vegetable garden whether or not they plan to compete.

It's fun to enter a contest, and it's even more fun to walk away with a ribbon and some prize money. Premiums are the monetary prizes awarded at the end of a contest, and most range from $1 to $50 for first place, less for second and third. In addition to the cash and ribbons for first (blue), second (red), and third (white) place, there may be other prizes donated by sponsors. These can include plaques, trophies, gardening products, garden-center gift cards, magazine subscriptions, and seeds. Additional awards might recognize Best of Show or Best of Class, Judges' Choice, Horticultural Excellence, or the person winning the most blue ribbons or the most prize money.

If ribbons, prizes, and a few bucks aren't enough incentive to enter a vegetable contest, consider chucking the ordinary vegetables to grow the oversized varieties. Giant pumpkin and cabbage contests offer premiums that can net contestants $1,000 or more for an especially weighty winner.

While some may think experienced gardeners have an edge on beginners, the simple act of gardening levels the field. Even time-tested gardeners have to find ways to cope with quirky weather, hungry insects, and plant

Field corn winners at
the Iowa State Fair

A 25-foot-tall replica of the couple
from Grant Wood's *American Gothic*

diseases. Gardeners may have to deal with tomatoes that drop their blossoms during a hot spell, cucumbers that grow a little crooked, or pumpkins that explode.

Other dangers may lurk in the garden, too. One of the most terrifying garden pests of all time was the Were-Rabbit that threatened the annual Tottington Hall Giant Vegetable Contest in the award-winning British feature film starring Wallace and Gromit.

If you're going to plant a vegetable garden anyway, you might as well take a shot at winning a prize. While many gardeners plan ahead for what they'll plant, grow, and show at the fair, others just wait to see what looks good in the garden on the day entries are due. Either strategy can work. As vegetable competitors in the United Kingdom like to say, "If you fancy it, why not give it a go?"

A FIRST TIME FOR EVERYONE

Some experts say beginners should start by competing in small community garden contests or at county fairs to gain experience exhibiting their vegetables. Some fairs encourage new competitors with a special division for first-time exhibitors.

A TEAM EFFORT

GINGER & CHUCK WERNER

AFTER MORE THAN 30 YEARS of competing in vegetable contests at the Iowa State Fair, Chuck and Ginger Werner know a thing or two about winning. They've lost track of their total prize money, and they keep all their ribbons in shoeboxes, but they still remember their very first prize: a fourth-place finish for ornamental corn.

Chuck's enjoyed going to the fair ever since he was a boy, missing only two while he was in the service. After settling into farming in Chelsea, Iowa, the couple thought they'd like to be part of the annual event by exhibiting their vegetables at the fair.

"For the first years we were just looking and making notes of which vegetables weren't entered or had just a few entries, and that's what we entered the next year," explains Ginger. "It's a sneaky way to enter because they usually place more than one or two, and we made notes of

"FOR THE FIRST YEARS WE WERE JUST LOOKING AND MAKING NOTES OF WHICH VEGETABLES WEREN'T ENTERED OR HAD JUST A FEW ENTRIES, AND THAT'S WHAT WE ENTERED THE NEXT YEAR."

—GINGER WERNER

which weren't very popular. We started getting ribbons and branched out from there."

One of their most memorable times at the fair was when three generations of the family competed at the same time and everyone went home with a ribbon. Another big year was when Ginger received the premier vegetable exhibitor's prize for winning the most premium money in the garden vegetable division. Chuck was runner-up.

The couple, married for more than 45 years, have always worked together as a team, even when going head-to-head with their vegetables. "We don't think of it as competing against each other, we use it to our advantage," Chuck says.

The potato class is a good example. Specimens are required to weigh between 6 and 12 ounces, so Chuck might enter an 8-ounce potato and Ginger a 12-ounce potato, doubling their chances of having a winning entry. "I just hope one or both of us will place," says Ginger.

Because every gardening season is different, every competition is different, too. Some years may be good for potatoes, but all the squash could be ruined by hail. The weather can also make or break a cucumber crop. As Chuck sees it, "one year there may be 30 or 40 plates of cucumbers at the fair and the next year, just 8 or 10. Mother Nature's the boss."

To prove his point, Ginger tells the story about a competitor they knew who grew only seven peppers one year, took five of them to the fair, and placed first. Another time, when there were several hundred peppers to choose from, none of

them placed. "It wasn't the right combination," she says. "You've got to be persistent. It takes time to get good at competing," adds Chuck.

Is there anything they wish they had known when they started entering vegetable contests? "How important maturity and uniformity are to the judges," says Chuck. "If you're showing green peppers, they all have to have the same number of lobes and be the same height and color. No insect damage, no scratches from handling. The more uniform they look, the better."

Make sure entries are fresh, Ginger advises. She recommends keeping produce refrigerated before the contest. She also suggests getting to the fair early on the morning of the contest to recut stems on entries like beets, peppers, and okra so they have a fresh, just-picked appearance.

When they're not competing, Chuck and Ginger are busy working their 320-acre farm and selling at two farmers' markets every week from May until October. They offer a variety of vegetables including potatoes, watermelons, peas, beans, cabbages, onions, squashes, poppping corn, and more. Ginger bakes fruit pies and yeast breads. Her dried three-pepper mix is an especially hot seller.

The fair remains an end-of-the-season celebration and social event for the couple. After so many years of competing, they've had the chance to get to know the other exhibitors and now it's like a big family, Chuck says. "There's a lot of work getting ready for the fair, but after the judging, we can just enjoy the rest of it. That's when the fun starts."

But don't let inexperience stop you from entering any event, especially if you have an exceptional crop to show off. As a judge once told me, "You've heard of beginner's luck, haven't you?"

Vegetable contests are annual events and an important part of state and county fairs. Sometimes contests for giant specimens — often pumpkins and cabbages — are held as separate, special events. Contests are usually scheduled at about the same time every year, typically during harvest time from July through October. To find a fair near you, call your county and state fair offices or search online. You can also look for fairs listed with local, state, and regional agricultural associations or check with the International Association of Fairs and Expositions.

Other options for vegetable competitions include local shows sponsored by garden clubs, garden centers, or community gardens. If you can't locate a contest in your area, suggest one. Contact your county's Cooperative Extension Service or Master Gardener's group to gauge interest in launching a new community event. Some groups start small with a single contest, a tomato tasting or giant vegetable contest, and grow from there.

Consider online photo contests, too. Some vegetable competitions are looking for beautiful contestants, but there are plenty of competitions for ugly or weird-looking fruits and vegetables. These contests may be sponsored by seed and plant companies, online magazines, or gardening websites. Online competitions typically ask gardeners to upload images of their entries and then award prizes to the winners.

AT THE TURN of the twentieth century, visitors to the California State Fair enjoyed viewing the bountiful exhibits of the state's prized fruits and vegetables almost as much as watching the spectacle of two full-sized locomotives crashing into each other.

STUDY *THE* SHOW BOOK

After finding the contest you want to enter, the next step is to get your hands on a copy of the show book, which may also be called the fair book, competitor's exhibition guide, or premium book. It contains everything you need to know for entering the contest: the competition schedule, contest rules, fees, deadlines, judging details, awards, and other show-specific information.

The show book provides specifics about the divisions, numbers, and classes (categories) of vegetables for open (adult) and junior (usually 18 and under) exhibits. Depending on the size of the event, there could be as many as 100 vegetable classes or just a dozen.

VEGETABLE CLASSES

Check to make sure there are classes for the vegetables you want to enter, and learn that contest's requirements for each class. This can save you the trouble of lugging a 3-foot-long Armenian cucumber to the fair only to find there's no category for a cucumber that size. There may be a number of special classes, like a collection of different garden vegetables or a single specimen plant such as a pepper.

Special Classes

Some competitions include classes for jumbo, novelty, and heirloom vegetables, too.

Jumbo. The rules for jumbo or giant vegetables explain how specimens will be measured. For example, an entry may be measured once around its midsection and once around from stem to blossom end. Judges may take the total of these two measurements to give the entry a score. For longest vegetables, like beans or gourds, judges may measure in a straight line from one end to the other. In case of a tie, the vegetables are usually weighed and the heavyweight declared the winner.

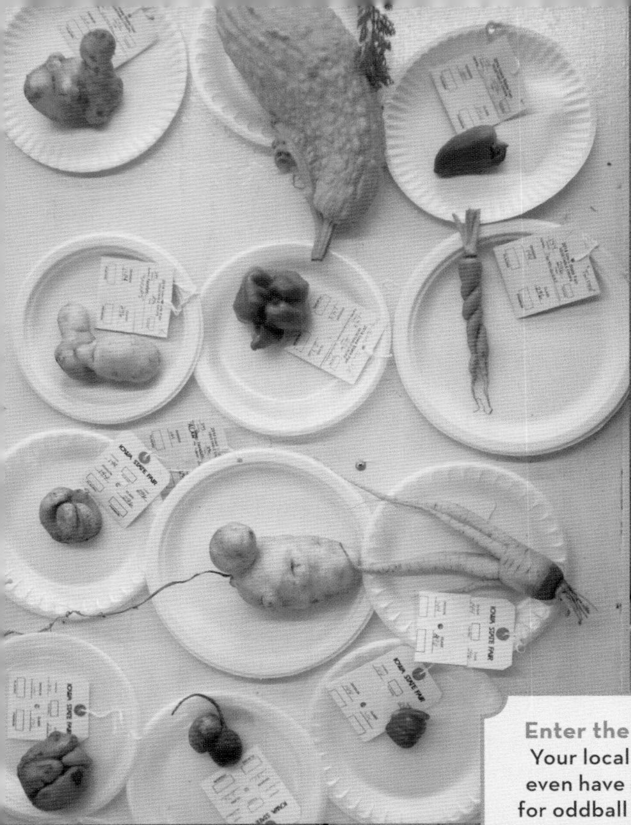
IOWA STATE FAIR
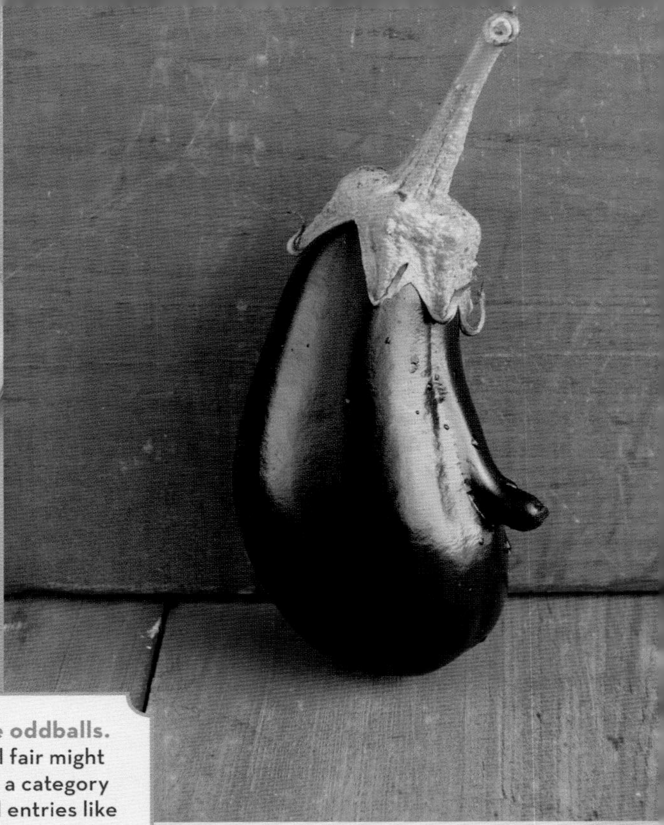

Enter the oddballs. Your local fair might even have a category for oddball entries like these, which might otherwise be considered the outcasts of the competition.

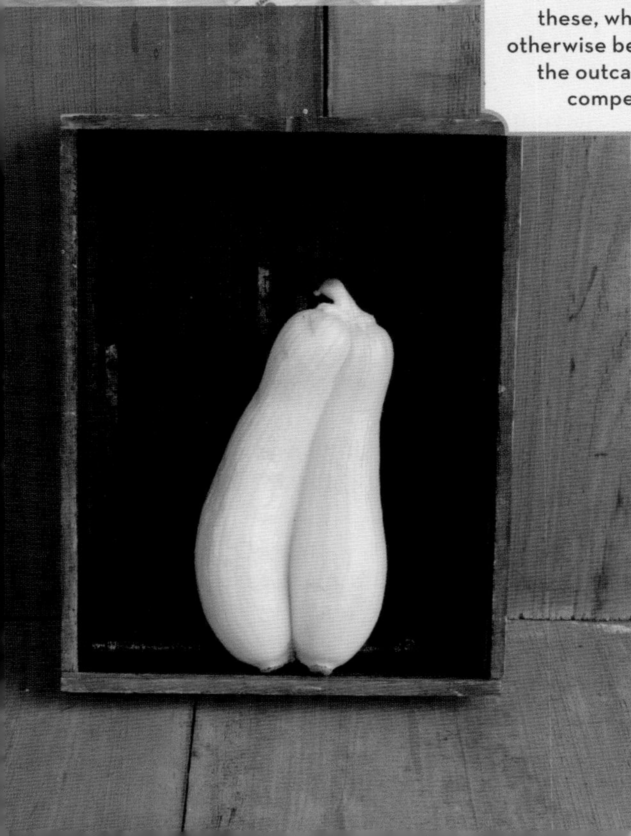
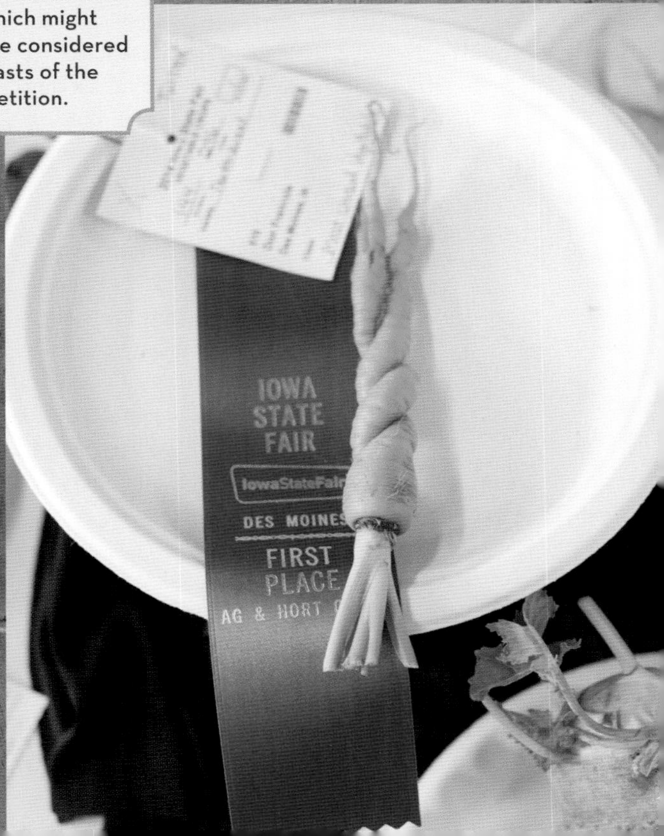
IOWA
STATE
FAIR
IowaStateFair
DES MOINES
FIRST
PLACE
AG & HORT

Jumbo cabbage

Regular size cabbage

Giant pumpkins are judged by weight alone, although there may be special awards for prettiest or ugliest.

Novelty. Novelty vegetables are those naturally occurring, strange-looking vegetables that crop up in gardens every now and then. Picture eggplants with noses, smiling tomatoes, potatoes with ears, and entwined carrots. Judges rate these oddities on their unusual appearance and comical qualities. Of course, the fair organizers have the right to deny entry to any anatomically correct vegetable that isn't appropriate for a general audience.

A SUPERSIZED EAR OF CORN at the 1852 Indiana State Fair gained fame for its 1,800 kernels from 30 rows that filled a 1.3-quart container.

Heirloom. If the fair has a category for heirloom varieties, the show book may define what constitutes an heirloom. One fair's rules specified an heirloom as "a vegetable from seed or stock that has been passed down within a family or community, or may be purchased seed or stock that's identified as an heirloom."

PLANNING FOR SUCCESS

The strategy for entering a vegetable contest is simple: plant and tend vegetables so you can harvest a certain number of picture-perfect specimens by showtime. It's easy enough to grow one flawless tomato or pick two prime peppers. The challenge is growing a beautifully matched set of vegetables that will be at their peak of perfection on show day.

As you may have discovered, vegetables don't always grow beautifully or according to schedule. In addition to competing against other gardeners, you're also competing against whatever Mother Nature throws your way. Weather can be too hot or too cold, too wet or too dry, or too windy; or thunderstorms can dump too much hail. A bad season of insect pests or other horticultural ailments can rudely disrupt your plans. That's why it's important to maintain control over all you can, starting way before the growing season.

Ginger and Chuck Werner collect miniature pumpkins for competition.

DO YOUR RESEARCH

As with any good project, planning is key. It pays to start thinking about the end of the season before the season actually begins. During the off-season, research the fruits and vegetables you want to grow. Read through seed catalogs and look for vegetable varieties with descriptors that signal potential prizewinners: *reliable*, *consistent*, *prolific*, *dependable*, *huge yields*, *delicious*, *flavorful*, and *good performer*. Look for regional information to help you find plants that will do especially well in your gardening area.

Select for reliability. You can prevent some plant problems by selecting fruits and vegetables bred to be disease-resistant. Plant breeders have spent years tinkering with vegetables so they'll grow well in different climates and produce consistent crops of good quality. Look for plants labeled as F_1, a first-generation hybrid that's the result of crossing two pure plant lines. Some popular examples of hybrids include 'Premium Crop' broccoli; 'Straight Eight' cucumbers; and 'Sungold', 'Better Boy', and 'Celebrity' tomatoes.

THE GARDENER VERSUS THE FUTURE FARMERS

WHEN I CALLED ABOUT ENTERING the vegetable competition at the Colorado State Fair, the clerk told me most competitors were members of clubs, but individual entries were welcome, too. When she said "clubs" I assumed she meant garden clubs.

Actually, the clubs are for teens, groups like 4-H and the National FFA Organization (also called Future Farmers of America). I didn't learn this until after I got up before dawn and drove 2 hours to get to the fair. I also discovered that these young competitors can enter the open classes as well as junior classes.

So there I was, the only adult competing against kids — and these kids were taking the competition very, very seriously. In addition to individual championship honors, a Best of Counties award was at stake.

I tried to remain invisible until my vegetable class was called. During the hot pepper competition, one of the young competitors pointed to my plate of 10 colorful and creatively arranged 'Mariachi' peppers. He asked, with more than a hint of surprise in his voice, "Did *you* grow *those*?"

That was right before the judge began shuffling the entries around the table as he inspected each and ranked them in order. For a brief moment, my peppers were first, before he moved them to the second-place spot.

To tell the truth, I was relieved to get out of there with a couple of red ribbons and some of my gardening dignity intact. I didn't mind at all losing to a future farmer.

'Contender' bush beans

Pick a winner. You can also look for varieties and cultivars that are known to be perennial winners. Take note of the winners at different contests, or ask other gardeners for their top suggestions. Seed or plant names may also offer clues to their winning qualities, like 'Prizetaker' leeks, 'First Prize' pumpkins, 'Contender' bush beans, and 'Nonna's Prize' tomatoes.

In a crowded field, unusual varieties might offer a better chance for success. At one county fair's hot pepper competition, I won a blue ribbon for entering a new pepper called 'Cayennetta'. My two fire-engine-red peppers stood out from the plates of green jalapeños, green Spanish 'Padron' peppers, and even a plate of green 'Bhut Jolokia' peppers (aka 'Ghost Chili', one of the hottest chile peppers in the world). Though judges have the option of tasting the entries, I noticed none of the hot pepper entries had been sampled.

KNOWING THE LINGO

BECAUSE SOME TERMS I'VE USED to describe plants may be confusing, here's a simple guide to help decipher them:

VEGETABLE OR FRUIT?

Throughout the book, I use the term *produce* to mean fruits and vegetables grown by home gardeners in backyards, front yards, farm gardens, community gardens, and small-space gardens. I sometimes use the word *vegetables* when talking about cucumbers, peppers, eggplants, tomatoes, squashes, and pumpkins — even though these are technically fruits, not vegetables. Instead of quibbling about whether to use the word *fruit* instead of *vegetable*, I've relied on how they're used in the kitchen. I understand tomatoes are technically fruits, but I'm not going to put them on my cereal and cover them with milk.

VARIETIES AND CULTIVARS

When discussing fruits and vegetables, the word *variety* often comes up. Varieties are groups of plants that were selected from the wild, and most varieties are *true to type*. That means seeds grown from varieties will have the same characteristics as the parent plant.

You'll also come across the term *cultivar*. *Cultivar* is short for *cultivated variety*. These are plants that are considered to have been tinkered with by human hands. Hybrids are a good example (even if you hear them called *hybrid varieties*). If grown from seed, cultivars typically produce a plant unlike its parent.

These days, gardeners seem to plant more cultivars than varieties, because more of them are widely available on the market. They're plants that have been bred to be more productive, have improved disease resistance, and — in some instances — are easier to grow.

SCHEDULE PLANTING DATES

Before the season starts, review the seed and plant descriptions. Pay attention to planting dates, number of days from germination to harvest, fertilizer requirements, spacing, and any given planting and growing information. Use the "days to harvest" as a guide so you'll have enough ripe produce to take to the contests you want to enter. Here are five tips for determining your prime planting dates:

• **Note days to maturity.** Look for the number of days (in the plant description or on the seed packet) required from planting seeds to harvesting the mature fruit or vegetable, sometimes listed as from transplanting to maturity. Remember that these dates are only approximations!

• **Check competition dates.** Make note of the dates of the vegetable competition. Check the show book for the first day of the fair or the day of judging for all the fairs you plan on entering. Most events are held in late summer or early autumn and at about the same time each year.

• **Count backward.** Start with the contest date and count back the number of days needed to grow each vegetable to maturity. This will give you an idea of your prime planting date.

Erik Francois and his dad, Don, use CAD-drawn maps of the garden to keep track of their vegetable varieties.

Harvesting for competition often means looking for the right number (as dictated by your local fair's guidelines) of similar-size vegetables.

- **Select additional dates.** Mark at least two additional planting dates, one a week or so earlier and one a week later, as "vegetable insurance" in case your crop ripens faster or slower than expected. This helps ensure you'll have enough ripe vegetables at contest time, regardless of the weather. Use succession planting for leafy green crops and herbs, planting seeds on a staggered schedule so you're sure to have a supply of mature specimens.

- **Plant more than you need.** Be sure to plant extra of each kind of vegetable so you'll have your choice of perfect specimens to take to the show.

GET READY ᵀᴼ SHOW

You've worked hard all season cultivating high-quality vegetables, so be just as diligent in harvesting, handling, transporting, and preparing them for the contest. To select your best entries, think like a judge. As one state-fair judge asked spectators looking at plates of tomatoes, "Which of these would you buy at the store?"

Whether searching the vegetable bins at a supermarket or sorting through produce at a farmers' market, discriminating shoppers look for the best of the bunch. So do judges. Prizewinners are usually the ones that match the market standard for ideal size, quality, and condition. Uniformity of specimens is also an important judging criterion.

HOW TO HARVEST

Before you pick, clip, or snip anything for the show, check the show book for specifics. Note the number and size of vegetables required for each class. Also check whether they need their stems and, if so, the length of each stem. If the guidelines for green beans specify 10 pods per plate, each the same length, with ½ inch of

stem, be sure to meet all those requirements. Use a ruler to measure and trim the stems.

Details count, and judges look for ways to sort the mediocre entries from the winners. You might miss winning a ribbon because a stem is too long or left on when it should be trimmed, or if for some other reason your exhibit fails to meet the show's basic standards for an entry.

Harvest only the best-looking, ripe vegetables. Each specimen should have an even color and be uniform in size, shape, color, and maturity; it should match the ideal type for the variety. There should be no blemishes, insect damage, or anything else that detracts from the entry.

And be prepared for the unexpected. Harvest a few extras of each, just in case something unfortunate happens on the way to the show.

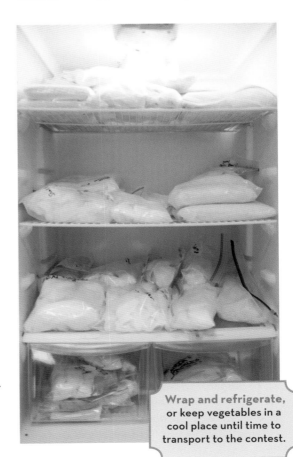

Wrap and refrigerate, or keep vegetables in a cool place until time to transport to the contest.

HOW TO PREPARE

Pick the produce as close to judging time as possible to prevent wilting or shriveling. Clean, but don't scrub, your harvest. Scrubbing with a brush may remove the bloom or otherwise detract from the vegetable's natural beauty. Rinse vegetables gently (briefly soak root vegetables), and use a soft cloth to remove any soil. Leaves can draw moisture away from the root, so trim tops from root vegetables when dug, saving some to retrim right before the judging. Wrap and refrigerate, or keep vegetables in a cool place until time to transport to the contest. Vegetables will store for several days in the refrigerator if wrapped in plastic and kept in the vegetable crisper.

To prepare large-leaved herbs like basil, cut stems the evening before and place in water to keep leaves fresh looking for the next day's judging. Leafy greens like lettuce and spinach do well when sprayed with water or dipped in water, or when stems are placed in water and then refrigerated.

HOW TO TRANSPORT

Pack your potential prizewinners carefully by wrapping them individually in newspaper, bubble wrap, tissue paper, or cloth. Then place them in sturdy containers (boxes or baskets) to prevent bruising during transport.

If you have a long drive to the fair, plan ways to keep your entries chilled during the drive. It's easy to wrap and place a small number of vegetables in a cooler with ice packs, but imagine the logistics of packing and transporting 50 entries, or trying to get a 1,000-pound pumpkin to a contest! Transporting a monster like that requires hours of planning, plenty of muscle power, and some very heavy equipment.

Wrap competing vegetables carefully — in damp paper towels, old socks, or whatever you've got — to get them to the fair. Be sure to trim stems to the length indicated by your fair's guidelines.

Fragile vegetables like long gourds require special support during transportation, to keep them from breaking.

AT THE SHOW

Every show is different, so be sure you know what you'll need once you arrive. Have the species name and the variety or cultivar name handy for each entry card. These details assist the judges, and they help educate fairgoers viewing the exhibits. In the early days of agricultural competitions, exhibitors were required to explain the type of seeds they planted, their methods of cultivation, how they raised their crops, and how the crops were harvested. You continue this tradition of agricultural education whenever you fill out entry cards with specimen specifics.

Most shows provide plain white paper plates with each exhibitor's number for displaying entries. Some competitors bring in exhibit boards, which look like wooden trays, to display their produce. The show book should specify display information. If it's unclear, either call ahead or pack some white paper plates, just in case.

If you're allowed to arrange your entries before the judging, prepare an eye-catching exhibit. Place the vegetables with all the stems facing the same way, if possible, and put smaller specimens on each end. Even though judging is based on the criteria for each class, presentation counts!

JUDGMENT TIME

The judging process is as varied as each event. At some fairs judging is closed, but other competitions invite contestants and the general public to stick around to watch and learn. The most helpful process, from a competitor's point of view, is an open one in which judges provide feedback to justify their choices and give advice for improving entries in the future.

Most horticulture contests have qualified and experienced judges who are either growers or industry professionals. Smaller contests may recruit fellow gardeners willing to volunteer their time. Whether judges are amateur or professional, their decision is final.

In most contests, judging is a blind process: you leave entries at the horticulture check-in table, where the clerks tag them and present them for judging. Although some might say it isn't proper vegetable showmanship for judges to see the exhibitor or the exhibitor's name

Judges spend considerable time examining the quality of each entry, looking for picture-perfect specimens that represent the market ideal for that vegetable class.

before judging is complete, some contests allow for face-to-face judging. In such contests, you wait for your vegetable classes to be called, present your vegetables, and then watch the judging.

TWO JUDGING SYSTEMS

Most fairs use the American System of judging for vegetable competitions. In the American System, judges rate each exhibit by comparing it to the other exhibits. Then each is ranked first, second, or third, with one ribbon color for each placing.

Another system of judging is called the Danish System. This system uses a set of standards to evaluate each entry on its own merit and assign it a numerical score. Ribbons are awarded based on the numerical scores. For example, blue ribbons may be awarded to entries that score 90 to 100 points. With this method, there may be more than one blue ribbon winner in each class.

WHAT JUDGES LOOK FOR

For the majority of contests following the American System, judges will be looking for the characteristics that make one entry stand out from the others. They'll be searching for the best set of perfect vegetables they've ever seen. For each entry, they'll be checking for the following:

- Correct number of specimens
- Uniformity in shape, color, and texture
- Premium quality on the outside and inside
- No blemishes or damage
- Stems present or absent, as specified
- True to type (specimen has all the characteristics of the variety or cultivar it claims to be)

To a certain degree, size matters, too. A plate of large tomatillos will probably top an entry that's just as perfect, but smaller. Unless you're entering a jumbo vegetable competition, though, avoid showing exceptionally enormous specimens; excessive size can signal they're overripe and past their prime.

VEGETABLE JUDGING COMMENT CARD

- ☐ Overmature
- ☐ Immature
- ☐ Undersized
- ☐ Oversized
- ☐ Needs grooming
- ☐ Blemished
- ☐ Wilted at judging
- ☐ Lack of uniformity among specimens
- ☐ Insect damage
- ☐ Lacking in quality:
  - ___ Form, shape
  - ___ Skin
  - ___ Flesh
  - ___ Color
  - ___ Taste
  - ___ Freshness
  - ___ Need to identify variety/species
  - ___ Other
  - ___ Judge's comments:

Some of the best advice for vegetable exhibitors dates back more than a century. A British vegetable expert named J. Wright revealed that judges always searched for faults and that the specimens with the fewest faults win the highest prizes. Quoted in an 1896 handbook for "amateurs, cottagers, and allotment-holders," he advised exhibitors to avoid mixing large and small specimens together because it weakens the exhibit. He also said that roots for the show table shouldn't be scrubbed with a hard brush, but washed with a soft brush or cloth. Wright suggested exhibitors who didn't win "should search calmly and patiently for the cause of the failure. The losers of today, who profit by experience and persevere, are the winners of the future."

THE RESULTS ARE IN

The show book should explain the timing of the awards ceremony and how winners claim their ribbons (and entries) when the fair ends. If you enjoyed participating and plan to enter again, write a few notes of what worked well for you and what you'd like to change for the next gardening season. Maybe it's the cultivars you plant, the classes you'd like to enter, or other ideas for creating a more successful experience.

At some fairs you may get back the form that the judges used to rate your entries. At one county fair I received a comment card for each entry, which included a list of 12 categories and a place for the judges' comments. The comments I received for my blue-ribbon basil were "Fairly uniform, large leaves, leaf quality is great! Taste is good!" Another county fair used a judging sheet that assigned points for quality, color, true to species, condition, and something called "the x factor." On that sheet I saw the judge's comments on my second-place 'Green Tiger' zucchini: "Beautiful color and perfect size, 7″ on the nose! Nice mild flavor and seeds aren't overdeveloped. x factor: Neat variety and congrats on picking at the perfect time." But there was room for improvement on my 'Suribachi' jalapeño pepper entry: "Very interesting variety; a little bit of decay in the seeds." My disappointment was tempered by winning a green ribbon for my description explaining how I grew these peppers organically.

Your own notes, plus comments from the judges, can improve your chances for ribbons, premiums, and prizes the next time around. It's also a good idea to take a look at the entries that took the top prizes. You might want to give those varieties a go next year.

A CORNSTALK measuring more than 16 feet won the Tall Corn Contest at the 1938 Indiana State Fair. Henry County resident Richard Jordan's entry was so tall that it reached the Administration Building's balcony.

Don Francois and his family — including brother-in-law Larry Dau (in the red cap) and brother Dave (not pictured) — have been competing against each other for the last eight years.

Fair volunteers ferry vegetable entries to the tables where they'll be judged.

CHAPTER 3

BLUE RIBBON BASICS

A PLANTING CHECKLIST

WHILE THE FOLLOWING CHAPTERS PROVIDE SPECIFICS FOR growing 10 different fruits and vegetables, this checklist is designed to give you an overview of how to grow champion produce. With these tips in hand, you're sure to grow a garden filled with quality specimens you'll be proud to take to any contest or at least to show off to friends and neighbors. And, by the way, best of luck!

☑ KNOW YOUR SOIL

The smart start for growing award-winning vegetables is to get your soil tested. A complete soil test, which involves taking samples and sending them to a lab, isn't difficult. It's worth the small effort to help you manage the nutrient and fertilizer needs of your prizewinning veggies. Just think, no more guessing.

A soil test provides you with the levels of the major nutrients — nitrogen, phosphorus, and potassium — and sometimes trace elements. It gives the pH level, which tells you whether your soil is alkaline (high pH), acidic (low pH), or neutral (just right). In dry regions where soils may contain high levels of salts, a good soil test will indicate the salinity of your soil samples. The results will help you amend the soil with the right nutrients.

☑ DIG IN WITH COMPOST

If you want to grow prizewinning fruits and vegetables, compost is your go-to organic soil amendment. Made from everyday household and yard waste, this rich, crumbly material improves soil structure and helps grow healthier plants.

Compost adds slow-release nutrients, helps the soil retain nutrients from added fertilizers, and helps maintain soil moisture. In fact, compost can be the answer to most gardening

Tomato plants grown in rich beds with good support will produce large quantities of high-quality fruits.

dilemmas, whether you garden in heavy clay soil or struggle with the sandy stuff. So dig in with compost to improve soil fertility, to encourage the beneficial critters in your soil, and to give your gardening efforts a boost in the process.

☑ PLANT IN THE SUNNIEST, SHELTERED SPOTS

Vegetable gardens need 6 or more hours of direct sun each day. With 5 hours, you can still grow most vegetables, but it's hard to produce prizewinners of anything except leafy greens. Find an area that's also protected from wind, if possible.

☑ PREPARE THE PLANTING BED

Vegetables grow best in loamy soil that contains lots of organic matter. Add a layer of organic matter like good-quality compost or well-aged manure (four or more months old, or purchase composted manure) to increase the soil's ability to hold moisture and nutrients. Organic matter will also improve the texture of sandy or clayey soils. Spread at least an inch of compost or other organic matter over the entire bed, even more for a new garden, if possible. Be sure to dig it in at least 6 to 8 inches deep. And, whatever you do, don't walk on the garden soil. Soil compaction limits root growth.

☑ NO VEGETABLE BED? NO PROBLEM!

Even if you don't have a big growing space, you can still grow and show beautiful specimens by planting in containers. Container gardens make it easy to control conditions, such as the amount of sun, water, and fertilizer each plant receives. Containers are portable so they can be scooted out of harm's way if bad weather such as hail is in the forecast.

For best results use 5- to 20-gallon containers with openings at least 12 inches wide; match the size of the container to the size of the mature plant. Be sure to punch or drill drainage holes in the container bottom, elevate slightly on bricks or blocks to aid drainage, and place a saucer underneath to protect patio or deck from water runoff.

Container options include wooden barrels, window boxes, flowerpots, washtubs, and even plastic buckets or bushel baskets. Clay pots are my least favorite for planting because the soil in these dries out faster than in plastic containers. If planting in a terra-cotta pot, try to provide some shade or plant in a plastic container hidden inside.

Mix in a slow-release fertilizer at planting time, because nutrients will wash right out of the pot from watering or drenching rainstorms. Water frequently to keep plants from drying out, and add a diluted fertilizer every few weeks through the growing season. Group containers close together to help prevent evaporation and to give the area the look of a real garden.

☑ MAKE THE MOST OF SHORT GROWING SEASONS

Your growing season is typically defined as the number of frost-free days you have for planting and growing. If you have a short growing season (like I do), you'll need to pay attention to the number of days to maturity for the fruits and vegetables you plant. You can also use season extenders (cold frames, plant protectors filled with water, high or low tunnels, and row cover) to get started sooner.

If you lack heat in the garden, make the most of your microclimates. Look for those naturally warmer areas of your growing space, such as the south-facing side of your house or next to a heat-absorbing fence or wall. Raised planting beds are also naturally warmer because all the sides are exposed. Planting in any of these ways can help you get a jump-start on the season.

☑ USE A SOIL THERMOMETER

A soil thermometer is a valuable but under-used tool that takes the guesswork out of when to plant. It's more reliable than planting by average frost dates or by the calendar. When used to measure soil temperature, a thermometer can give you the go-ahead to plant cool-season crops when the soil warms to an optimum 35 to 40°F. It can stop you from planting peppers before the soil has warmed to the 55 or 60°F needed for these heat-lovers to grow well.

☑ BUY GOOD-QUALITY PLANTS ᴼᴿ START FROM SEEDS

If you purchase transplants, look for the healthiest plants with stocky stems and without any fruit already formed. Make sure transplants have been well tended; look for moist soil and nicely formed roots. Healthy transplants makes for a healthier garden.

If you want to grow unusual varieties, you'll probably need to start them from seeds. In some areas, seeds for plants like tomatoes and peppers need to be started indoors, allowing plenty of time for plants to get to the transplant stage in advance of the con-test. Other seeds, like squash seeds, are sown directly into the garden by following the

planting instructions on seed packets. It's important to follow the spacing recommendations, too.

Some seeds, like those for beans and cucumbers, germinate faster if they're soaked in water overnight. If you don't see seedlings after a week or so, plant again right away.

☑ ACCLIMATE BEFORE PLANTING

Tender plants, like tomatoes, need time to get conditioned to the outdoors before planting. Move plants outside and expose them to sun slowly, over the course of about a week before planting, so delicate leaves and stems have a chance to toughen up before planting.

One of the tricks I use to prevent transplant shock after planting is to cover each plant with a 1-gallon plastic milk jug with the bottom cut off. I place the jug over each plant with the

Tender plants like tomatoes should be hardened off before they're planted out in the garden.

Don Francois's
lush Iowa garden

spout end up and the cap removed to allow air flow. After three days, I remove these miniature greenhouses and let nature take over.

☑ GROW A HEALTHY GARDEN

The healthier your plants are, the fewer insect pests and plant diseases you'll see. Use good cultural practices like selecting vigorous, disease-resistant cultivars, rotating crops, giving plants plenty of room for air to circulate, and timing plantings to avoid pests. Quickly remove any diseased plants and put them in the trash, not the compost pile.

Plan ahead for controlling insect pests early in the season to give young plants the healthiest start possible. Cooperative Extension horticultural agents or Master Gardeners can advise you on the specifics of when to plant to avoid pest infestations at the beginning of the season for your region. After that, keep an eye on the garden so you can catch problems early and take action.

It's also important to keep your garden weed-free. Not only does it make for a more attractive garden, but your vegetable plants won't have to compete with weeds for nutrients and water. Weeds also provide safe harbor for problem insects.

☑ WATER CONSISTENTLY BASED ᴏɴ PLANT NEEDS

Plants grow best when they receive consistent water that goes deep into the soil. Unless your garden receives an inch or so of rain each week, you'll need to irrigate. Drip irrigation makes it easy to get moisture directly to plant roots without wetting leaves to prevent foliar diseases like powdery mildew. Check to make sure water

soaks into the soil at least 5 inches deep. Stick your finger deeply into the soil to check whether the soil is cool and moist. This type of deep watering is especially important when plants are forming roots and fruits. Adequate water makes for large, high-quality specimens.

Never let the garden dry out. During the heat of summer, plants may need watering more frequently than at the beginning of the season. A soil moisture meter can help you decide when it's time to water, but using your finger is cheaper.

Overwatering can cause as much of a problem as underwatering. Plants don't like to grow in soggy soil. For example, too much water while tomatoes are ripening can reduce the sugar content and affect flavor.

Competition-
worthy vegetables
come from plants
that are healthy,
well tended, and
relatively pest-free.

☑ ENCOURAGE PREDATORS

Plant for beneficial insects that target insect pests. Lady beetles (ladybugs), lacewing larvae, and spiders are some of the beneficial insects that help control pest populations. To attract beneficial insects to your yard, plant a diverse landscape with layers from low-lying groundcovers to evergreen and flowering shrubs. Plant flowers in your vegetable patch, too. Grow some that bloom from early in the season to mid-season and late in the season. Good choices include alyssum, dianthus, larkspur, viola, black-eyed Susan, borage, lovage, lavender, salvia, sunflower, and zinnia. The more insects in the landscape, the more insect predators you'll have, including birds.

☑ TRY SIMPLE STRATEGIES ꜰᴏʀ PEST CONTROL

There are many ways to outsmart the pests that pester your plants. Handpick and destroy large pests like tomato hornworms. Knock beetles into a jar of soapy water, where they'll drown. Spray a forceful stream of water on both sides of leaves to dislodge aphids and spider mites. Trap slugs in a shallow dish filled with beer. Or deter slugs with irritants like coffee grounds, dryer lint, or other abrasive substances placed around the base of plants. Diatomaceous earth is especially abrasive; this powdery substance is the remains of fossilized microorganisms. Sprinkle it on or around plants to discourage slugs, snails, grubs, flea

beetles, and other pests. Use sticky traps to lead tiny leafhoppers, thrips, and aphids to their demise.

Row cover cloth is an excellent physical barrier, especially when tied down tightly so insects can't crawl inside. Cutworm collars, like plastic cups or juice cans with the ends removed, prevent the hungry critters from crawling up plant stems.

Marigolds help control nematodes, those harmful microscopic pests, by secreting a substance through their roots. Plants that are susceptible to nematode damage, like tomatoes, benefit when marigolds are planted nearby.

☑ USE BIOLOGICAL CONTROLS WHEN POSSIBLE

You can enlist living organisms to help you grow your vegetables. Called biological controls, these bacteria, fungi, and beneficial nematodes target certain pests without harming birds or pets. One of the best known is *Bacillus thuringiensis* (Bt), a soil bacterium that helps control caterpillars and beetle larvae, if the right kind is applied at the right time. Beneficial nematodes are effective against grubs and cutworms.

Use chemical controls only as a last resort. Before using any chemicals, natural or synthetic, read the label carefully and follow instructions. Make sure the product is safe for beneficial insects. Organic controls include insecticidal soaps, horticultural oils, and repellents such as neem oil.

☑ FOLLOW FERTILIZER GUIDELINES

For high-quality produce you may need to fertilize once a month, especially during the prime growing season. Use the fertilizer of your choice or a recommendation from your favorite gardener. Some prefer fish emulsion and seaweed extract; others use fruit- or vegetable-specific organic formulas. There are many all-purpose water-soluble plant foods on the market, too. Whatever you use, follow the recommended rates of application (or dilution, for liquid formulas). Too much fertilizer makes plants more attractive to pests and can interfere with fruit production (and your tomatoes won't taste as good). The key is to keep plants well fed.

☑ PREPARE FOR NEXT SPRING

Prepare garden beds in fall to anticipate the next growing season. Layer leaves, compost, and fertilizer on the bed, and then turn under into the soil. You can also dig trenches in the beds; pile in compost, dry leaves, and fertilizer; and cover these with soil. The compost and leaves will decompose and leave the soil more fertile for spring. Some gardeners plant cover crops like winter rye, hairy vetch, or clover to boost soil organic matter and fertility.

☑ KEEP GOOD RECORDS

Record what you plant and when, how each plant performed, and the yield or numbers you harvested. Also note what inputs you added (what type of fertilizer, how much, and when you applied it). Jot down problems with weather, insects, and diseases; note your solutions and their results. Use the information to make good planting choices for the next season of vegetable contests.

CHAPTER 4

BEANS

BEANS ARE A WONDERFUL VEGETABLE FOR BEGINNERS TO take to the fair, because they're so easy to grow. It's a snap to win ribbons for fresh beans by selecting varieties that promise loads of picture-perfect pods. If you want to plant the most versatile of these vegetables, try the French garden bush bean. It can be shown as a snap bean, green shelling bean, and even a dry bean.

PULSES, THOSE EDIBLE DRIED seed crops of the legume family, are some of the oldest cultivated foods. They've been the heartbeat of healthy eating for thousands of years. It doesn't seem quite right to simply call them beans.

Experts may disagree on where, how, and by whom beans were domesticated, but they all recognize beans are one of the world's most important food crops. The common bean that most gardeners grow (*Phaseolus vulgaris*) probably originated in the Americas, as did the runner bean (*Phaseolus coccineus*), the lima or butter bean (*Phaseolus lunatus*), and the tepary bean (*Phaseolus acutifolius*).

Fava (*Vicia faba*), or broad beans, are a different part of the legume family and probably originated in the Mediterranean, most likely in ancient Egypt. Hyacinth beans (*Lablab purpurea*, aka *Dolichos lablab*) and cowpeas (*Vigna unguiculata*) came to us from Africa. Adzuki beans (*Vigna angularis*) and soybeans (*Glycine max*) probably originated in China.

The United States is one of the largest producers of snap beans, and Americans eat hundreds of millions of pounds each year. Market demand has led to improved traits that consumers and gardeners appreciate: smooth, straight, and stringless pods; slow-developing seeds; disease resistance or tolerance; and uniformity in color, shape, and length. All these qualities are important to the competitive bean grower, too.

Green, yellow, and purple snap beans are some of the most popular beans planted in home gardens today. New cultivars include dwarf plants with full-size beans; bush plants with upright habits; plants that thrive in short seasons; and beans that provide bigger yields, slimmer pods, deeper colors, improved flavor, improved disease resistance, and whatever else gardeners want. Despite the continuing new bean blitz, there are still plenty of heirloom varieties that will never go out of style.

BEST BETS FOR BEANS

HERE ARE SEVEN All-America Selections beans that might be winners in your garden. The dates in parentheses give the year they were selected as winners.

- 'Cherokee Wax' bush bean (1948)
- 'Derby' bush bean (1990)
- 'Fordhook 242' lima bush bean (1945)
- 'Goldcrop' wax bush bean (1974)
- 'Kentucky Blue' pole bean (1991)
- 'Mascotte' French filet bush bean (2014)
- 'Topcrop' bush bean (1950)

BEAN BASICS

If you don't know beans about beans, let's boil it down to the basics. Beans are an easy-to-grow warm-season vegetable that can be eaten fresh or dried for storage. The distinction between types of beans depends upon where they are in their stage of development when gardeners pick them, and on their growth habits.

- **Snap beans** are grown for their fresh pods that hold immature or undeveloped seeds. Some people call these string beans, even though the term went out of fashion when stringless beans were introduced more than 100 years ago. Snap beans can grow on bush plants or pole plants. They include green beans, filet beans (aka haricot verts), Romano beans, and yellow wax beans.

- **Green shelling or horticultural beans** are grown for their mature, fresh seeds, which are removed from their pods. These include

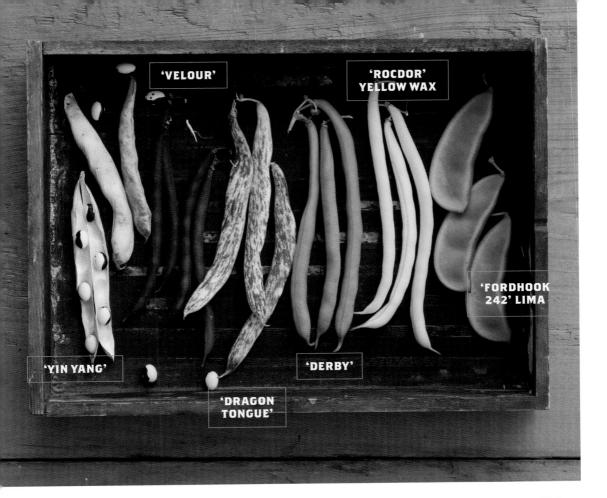

'VELOUR'

'ROCDOR' YELLOW WAX

'FORDHOOK 242' LIMA

'YIN YANG'

'DERBY'

'DRAGON TONGUE'

BEANS IN EVERY GARDEN

FRESH BEANS HAVE BEEN one of the most popular vegetables for generations. As early as 1799, Philadelphia's D. Landreth Seed Company listed 11 varieties of beans in its catalog. These included 'Cranberry', 'Red-Speckled Valentine', and 'Broad Windsor' bush beans; 'Carolina Sieva' lima beans; and 'Scarlet Runner' pole beans. As gardens grew, so did the choices for beans. In his 1917 vegetable gardening guide, New York gardener Ralph Lyon recommended his preferred tools, fertilizer, seeds, and plants. He listed one packet of 'Burpee's Stringless Green Pod' bush beans as a garden essential.

All-America Selections (AAS) picked up where Ralph left off by recommending 'Asgrow Stringless Green Pod' and 'Black Valentine' in 1933. Those two were the first of nearly 40 beans the organization has tested and suggested to gardeners over the years.

broad beans (fava beans), lima beans, and flageolet beans.

- **Dry shelling beans** are those grown to the mature seed stage and allowed to dry in their pods before being harvested for storing. Dry beans are especially attractive with many dark, rich colors or striped and speckled seeds. Examples of dry shelling beans include kidney, navy, pinto, black turtle, and cranberry beans.

- **Bush beans** (also called determinate varieties) are easy to grow because plants produce all their beans at about the same time, in as little as 45 days from planting. With their bushy habit, they grow about 24 inches tall and just as wide. Bush beans rarely need support unless it's to help keep pods from touching the ground or to keep plants upright in areas prone to strong winds.

- **Pole beans** (also called indeterminate varieties) mature later than bush beans and produce more beans over a longer period of time. As their name suggests, pole (or runner) beans are twining forms that grow on long vines that need poles or other upright supports. They take longer to mature than bush beans (typically 90 days or more).

- **Half-runner beans** (also called semi-determinate) grow on bushy plants. They form tendrils like other runner beans, but don't grow as tall.

Hundreds of beans could make nice specimens for a vegetable competition. To narrow the long list, decide which bean classes you want to enter and look for varieties that match the length of season for your region. If you're a bean beginner, start with bush snap beans because they grow quickly (45 to 60 days) and you don't have to install poles or other supports.

Select cultivars that grow high yields of uniform beans and offer disease resistance

CHECKLIST FOR BLUE RIBBON DRY SHELLING BEANS

SOME FAIRS INCLUDE A CLASS for dry shelling beans. Contests typically require a certain amount of matching beans, from 1 cup to 1 quart. Your show-off beans should be just like the dry beans you buy at the grocery store or farmers' market; you can tell if they're thoroughly dry when they resist a fingernail trying to pierce the hard seed coat. Measure carefully, and ensure that no moisture, mold, chaff, or foreign objects are mixed in with your beans.

PICK
- ☐ Market-perfect, hard and dry beans
- ☐ Bean color is true to type
- ☐ Uniform in size and shape

PASS
- ☐ Soft, rubbery, or moldy beans
- ☐ Beans that vary in size, shape, or color
- ☐ Damaged or chipped beans

PRESENT
- ☐ Wipe beans with a soft cloth; don't wash
- ☐ Weigh or measure beans accurately

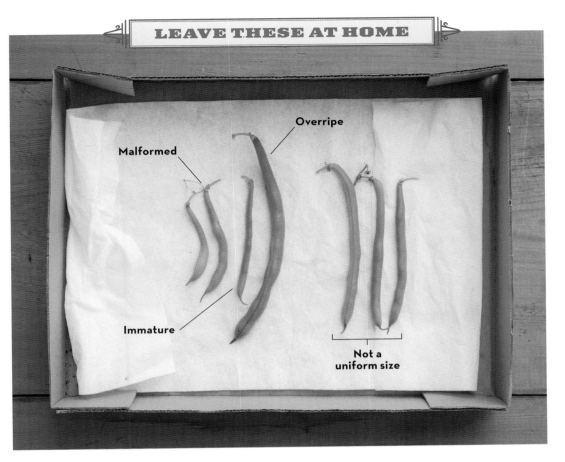

Overripe

Malformed

Immature

Not a
uniform size

or some disease tolerance. Most importantly, plant the beans you and your family will want to eat. In a good year, you may be harvesting bushels of beans well before the contest!

In the late 1800s, vegetable exhibitions typically included classes for broad beans, French beans, and runner beans. These days there may be many more classes that include fresh beans (green snap, yellow wax, purple, and Italian), shelled beans (like limas), and dry shelling beans.

Contest rules will specify the number of identical fresh pods (12 to 25) or the size of the container for dried beans (cup, pint, or quart). If you're planting dry shelling beans, you may need more plants and you'll need to allow four to six weeks longer for them to mature and dry.

PLANTING ⚡ THE BEST BEANS

Growing beans is simple if you keep in mind the environmental problems that affect them. Beans are sensitive to extremes during their different stages of growth, so plan ahead. Consider how to use the following information to grow the best beans possible in your region.

Cold and heat. The majority of beans, especially limas, need warmth to germinate. So wait to plant until your soil warms to about 50°F and weather is 60 to 85°F. As an alternative, warm the garden bed by covering with black plastic before planting, and protecting with row cover after planting.

ENGINEERING FOR VEGETABLE SUCCESS

DON FRANCOIS

IT DOESN'T TAKE THE MIND OF AN ENGINEER to enter more than 100 classes of vegetables at the state fair, but it certainly helps. It also helps to be well organized, be handy with spreadsheets, and have an army of friends willing to help at the end of the season. That's how Don Francois of Des Moines, Iowa, has managed to become one of the top vegetable exhibitors at the Iowa State Fair year after year.

Don is in agriculture-based engineering; he designs processing facilities that clean and package seeds for some of the biggest names in the business. Most of his work is with processing corn, soybeans, and wheat seeds, but he also works on equipment designed for processing vegetable seeds.

No wonder he's able to apply the same kind of engineering precision to his garden. The maps of

his garden, created with computer-aided design software, are works of art. Each map is precisely detailed with the crop he's growing, the variety he planted, and the planting date. For some crops he also notes the theoretical ready date, based on the number of days to harvest.

Don's garden evolved slowly from 1999, when he decided to enter a few vegetables in the fair. Together, he and his oldest son, Ryan, took a modest 12 entries to the competition. Over the course of just a few years, the number of his entries grew significantly. For the last seven years he's entered more than 100 classes at the fair. In August 2014 he set a personal record with 134 entries!

Don goes for quality as well as quantity. He's won 10 trophies for winning the most prize money,

as either the top exhibitor or the runner-up. His wife, Denise, has said she could make a quilt out of the 80 to 100 ribbons he collects every year.

Don grew up on a farm in northeast Iowa and had some experience with vegetable competitions while in 4-H. He hadn't gardened for years until four empty raised beds near his office got him itching to get his hands dirty again.

Now the garden includes 13 raised beds that have spilled into a neighboring field. Don estimates he cultivates less than ⅛ acre of total gardening space, but it's designed to yield maximum results.

What started as a gardener's summertime hobby is now an extraordinary 10-month process, and Don has it down to a fine science. He starts

WHEN THE CROP IS READY, "HARVEST EVERY OTHER DAY BECAUSE BEANS CAN GO FROM TENDER TO LUMPY IN A COUPLE OF DAYS."

— DON FRANCOIS

in January by planning the upcoming season. By February he's spending his nights reading seed catalogs and looking for new introductions. In March he starts about 250 cells of seeds — tomatoes, peppers, cabbages, and broccoli and grows them under lights. As soon as he can work the ground in spring, he tills an area for planting onions. He says it's important to get onion plants in the ground by the first of April, or there won't be any big onions to take to the fair.

Just like his grandfathers, Don always plants potatoes on Good Friday, no matter where the holiday falls on the calendar. It's such a tradition that folks at his work joke about it, saying the only

reason he gives them the day off is just so he can plant potatoes.

From April to the middle of June, Don is busy planting his prizewinning garden. He buys some vegetables as transplants and fills in the rest of the garden by sowing seeds directly in the beds. Everything is carefully timed, based on the vegetable's maturity date and aiming for prime condition for the state fair. He may grow several cultivars of each class of vegetables, so he'll have enough at just the right time. For example, in the snap bean classes he'll plant several different kinds; whichever is ready at fair time, that's what he'll exhibit.

"Every year is different, especially for beans," he explains. "You'll want to plant beans very thick, thicker than the packet says, because there can be germination problems." He advises bean growers to keep the soil moisture even and to ensure the beans don't dry out. When the crop is ready, "harvest every other day because beans can go from tender to lumpy in a couple of days," he says.

The days and nights before the fair can be long ones, culminating in an annual party the Monday before Tuesday's vegetable judging. That's when friends gather at his house to help sort through the bushels of potential prizewinners.

Don says his reward isn't about the trophies or ribbons or prize money. It's about the personal satisfaction of growing his own food. "I love the challenge of seeing something and wondering if I can grow it. My wife will tell you I'm overly competitive, that I just have a competitive nature," he says. "But it's the excitement of watching the garden grow and seeing it be successful. Plus we eat very well, as you can imagine."

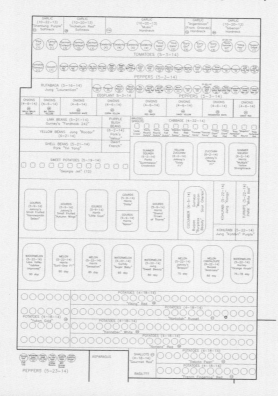

Don's CAD drawing of his garden

In the days before the fair, Don's friends and family all show up to help harvest and sort the vegetables.

CHECKLIST FOR BLUE RIBBON SNAP BEANS

ARE YOUR BEANS READY for prime time? Judges will be looking for the precise number of well-formed pods (either round or flat) that are at the perfect stage for eating or preserving — tender, firm, succulent, and stringless. Harvest only beans that pass the snap test: a sample bean pod should snap cleanly when broken in half. Use scissors to carefully snip pods from the plant; all should be the same length with some stem remaining. If pods are a little curved, snip from the plant, wrap in a wet paper towel, and bend gently to straighten before the contest.

PICK
- ☐ Straight, round pods
- ☐ Proper color for maturity (green, or golden yellow for wax beans)
- ☐ Seeds small and undeveloped
- ☐ Uniform in size, length, and color

PASS
- ☐ Pods with large seeds
- ☐ Odd pods, crooked pods, pods of different sizes
- ☐ Soft spots, voids, damage, rust, cracks
- ☐ Poorly trimmed beans

PRESENT
- ☐ Clean pods by wiping with a soft cloth
- ☐ Trim stems to specified length
- ☐ Arrange by size on the plate, like a fan

Waiting for warm weather also helps prevent root rot and damping off. Unlike most beans, broad (fava) beans prefer cool temperatures and can be planted in cool spring soil. If you're planting dry beans in a cooler climate, look for short-season types and plan ways to extend the season for maximum warmth and sunlight.

Time your plantings so pods form during more moderate temperatures. Excessive heat and drying winds while beans are flowering and pods are developing can result in blossom drop, poor fruit set, or malformed pods.

Soil fertility and acidity. Beans may be a nitrogen-fixing legume, but they still require fertile soil. To minimize disease problems, grow in quick-draining soil. A well-amended, fluffy soil helps seeds germinate and sprout quickly. Prepare the garden bed by digging in organic matter and a moderate amount of a well-balanced fertilizer to give plants a good start. A neutral to slightly acidic soil pH is ideal; extremely high or low soil pH can impair crop quality and yield.

Avoid water stress. Beans are insistent when it comes to water, requiring about 1 inch a week, especially when plants are forming pods and seeds. Don't let the soil dry completely between waterings, because drought or water stress can reduce the number of flowers and pods, and the pods that do form may be misshapen, tough, or stringy. But don't go overboard.

A trellis made out of hog panels helps direct the growth of the plant up and over.

Overwatering can promote root rot and stunt plant growth, too.

SOWING FOR SHOWING

Pick a sunny spot to grow your beans. You don't need to start them indoors; sow them outdoors once soils have warmed. The timing varies depending on the beans you're planting. To make sure fast-growing bush beans will be at the peak of perfection for the contest, you may need to plant successive crops at two-week intervals. Count the number of warm days until the contest and match to the maturity dates for the beans you want to show.

Some gardeners coat bean seeds with an inoculant immediately before planting to supply the beneficial bacteria (*Rhizobium*) that fix nitrogen. These bacteria live in nodules that form on roots of legumes; they take nitrogen from the air and "fix" it into a form that plants can use. As an alternative, some seed companies sell bean seeds pre-inoculated with the matching rhizobacteria. Benefits to inoculation include improved germination, stronger plants, and bigger yields.

When planting bush beans, space rows 2 to 3 feet apart. Plant seeds 4 to 6 inches apart in the rows. Before planting pole beans, set up trellises or teepees in the garden. Devise a vertical system that fits your garden to keep vines and beans healthy. I've seen chain-link fences, nylon or trellis netting, and wire strung between branches or recycled poles to support pole beans. Plan ahead and place the supports so beans will be easy to harvest without trampling other plants in the garden.

Pole beans need a helping hand to find their poles. Train plant tendrils to climb the supports as soon as plants are 6 to 7 inches tall. Keep weeds away from bean plants (and maintain even soil moisture) with an organic mulch. Good options include dry untreated lawn clippings or shredded leaves (run over with a lawn mower). Because the roots of bean plants are

shallow, take extra care when weeding and avoid deep cultivation. Either weed by hand or carefully clip off weed heads.

GROWING GREAT BEANS

Beans won't need much (if any) fertilizing after planting, especially if the soil was well amended with organic matter ahead of time. In fact, over-fertilizing can stunt plant growth or cause excessive leafy growth with just a few bean pods. Lightly fertilize after the first harvest for increased bean yields and improved vegetable quality.

When watering your bean patch, keep the story of Goldilocks and the three bears in mind. The soil shouldn't be too wet or too dry, but just right. Aim for about 1 inch of water each week, especially once plants start flowering, forming buds, and setting pods. If you notice blossoms or pods dropping, or plants forming misshapen pods, plants are getting either too much or too little water. Wet leaves provide breeding grounds for disease, so water in the morning and at ground level to keep foliage dry. Avoid touching wet vines to prevent spreading foliar diseases.

HARVESTING PRIZEWINNERS

No matter what kinds of beans you've planted, when it's time to harvest, look for pods that are considered the market ideal. Here is what to look for.

Snap beans. These beans grow and mature quickly, so harvest pods almost daily to encourage vines to keep producing. Use clippers to snip pods from vines when they reach competition size (4 to 8 inches) and are well filled with small seeds. Beans are ripe when you can snap them easily. Remove any beans that are bendy, wrinkly, or overmature (seeds have swollen inside pods).

Harvest as close to the contest as you can. If necessary, store beans in the refrigerator for three to four days in an airtight (moisture-proof) container. Don't wash before storing,

Don Francois and his crew sort green beans to find ones that are similar sizes.

Don Francois gently massages beans that are slightly too curved to optimize their shape for display in competition.

because this can cause pods to decay. If refrigerated too long (more than a few days), beans will start to toughen.

Fresh shelling (horticultural) beans.
Harvest only plump, firm pods. Split open a few sample pods to make sure beans are mature and at the peak of freshness. If beans have tough skins, they were left on the vine too long. Keep checking beans as pods start to mature and change color from green to yellow.

Dry shelling beans.
As dry beans mature, cut back on watering. Dry beans will be ready to harvest when most of the leaves turn yellow and drop. You'll know when beans are dry because they'll rattle when you shake pods, or some pods will start to split.

Clip pods (or pull up the entire plant) to keep them dry and prevent mold. Beans may need additional time under cover to dry thoroughly before shelling.

Because shelling beans may not be dry in time for an August contest, gardeners who show dry beans "shell out" their beans in fall and then store the dry beans to exhibit the following year. Once beans are separated from their dry pods, sort and store in glass jars.

One shelling method is to crack open the pods with your hands; the dry beans will sink to the bottom of a bowl, ready for sorting. Other methods include placing pods in a burlap sack or pillowcase and gently crushing them to free beans. Then use a fan, stiff breeze, or air compressor to help blow the pods away from beans as you drop them into a bucket or bowl.

CHECKLIST FOR BLUE RIBBON FRESH SHELLING BEANS

FRESH SHELLING BEANS and lima beans may be shown shelled or unshelled, depending on the requirements at the fair. If you shell them, make sure all beans are at their most tender stage for eating and uniform in color, shape, size, and maturity. Wait to pick and shell right before show-time, or refrigerate in an airtight container for just a few days. If exhibiting unshelled specimens, pick before seeds become overmature, and display your entry like high-quality, fresh snap beans.

PICK
- ☐ Mature pods of uniform size, shape, and color
- ☐ Well-developed beans inside pods
- ☐ Beans tender and fresh, with a bright color
- ☐ Stems trimmed to required length

PASS
- ☐ Wilted, flabby, yellow, or dried pods
- ☐ Pods that vary in color
- ☐ Misshapen pods, poorly filled pods, hard or brittle beans
- ☐ Pods damaged from rust or insects

PRESENT
- ☐ Wait until right before showtime to pick and shell
- ☐ Clean with a soft dry cloth (don't wash)
- ☐ Sort seeds by age (don't mix young with overmature)

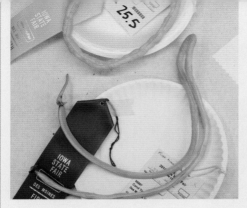

GOING FOR LENGTH

THE FOLKS VISITING the 1921 Minnesota State Fair had the chance to see the 37-inch winner of the longest string bean contest. That's a long bean, but they can grow longer! A North Carolina gardener grew a 48-inch runner bean in 1994.

If there's a long bean contest in the jumbo vegetable competition at your fair, here's how to try for a new record. Start with the right kind of seeds, and sow twice as many as you think you'll need. Build a supersturdy, extra-tall support that will allow beans to hang freely and prevent curling. Prune off any side shoots to leave one main runner. Hand-pollinate to ensure there will be plenty of full pods to choose from. (For more on this technique, see Sex and the Single Cucumber, page 107.) Remove most beans when they're very small; leave only the two best beans to grow on. Feed with a balanced fertilizer every two weeks. Clip long beans from the vine a day or so before the contest.

A few beans to try include 'Yard Long' (30 inches), 'Liberty' (20 inches), 'Enorma' (20 inches), and 'Red Noodle' (18 inches). Read bean descriptions to make sure there's enough time for your chosen variety of long bean to reach its full potential.

BEATING BEAN PROBLEMS

Beans are easy to grow for most folks. You can prevent many problems by cultivating a healthy garden. Rotate where you plant bean crops every two to three years, because bean diseases can lie dormant in the soil for several years. Plant in warm soil, and sow healthy seeds of varieties that are disease resistant or tolerant to anthracnose, bean mosaic virus, rust, curly top virus, or the bean diseases most common in your region.

Space plants so there's good air circulation. Don't use overhead sprinklers to water plants. Keep leaves as dry as possible, and don't work in the garden or harvest beans when foliage is wet. If you see diseases developing, carefully remove infested plants right away. Be sure to wash your hands and clippers to keep from spreading problems to other plants.

Depending on your region of the country, you may have to deal with one or more of the following bean problems in your garden. However, it's likely you'll still have a few nice pods to take to the fair.

- **Seedlings that disappear overnight?** Cutworms are the likely culprit. These small, fat caterpillars can fell stems of small seedlings or climb stems and feed on leaves. Prevent cutworm feeding by placing round cardboard tubes, plastic cups, or other cutworm collars around plant stems to foil their efforts.

- **Leaves that look like skeletons?** The Mexican bean beetle is probably at work. Look for adults that resemble large yellow or orange ladybugs and their fuzzy yellow-to-orange larvae, which cause the leaf damage. Time your planting either earlier or later to avoid the initial onslaught. Or use row cover, tightly anchored along the edges, to

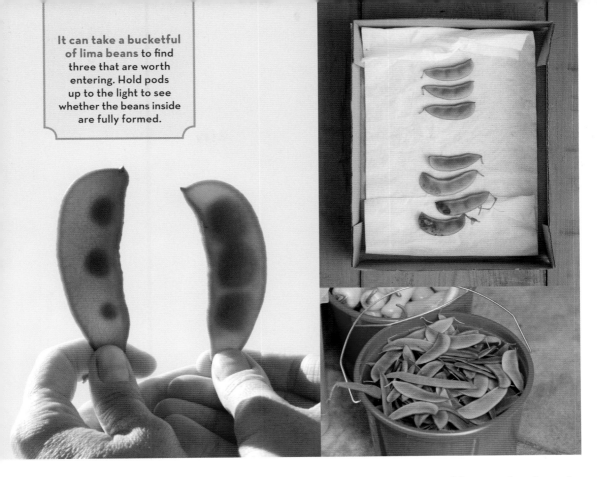

It can take a bucketful of lima beans to find three that are worth entering. Hold pods up to the light to see whether the beans inside are fully formed.

exclude beetles. (Remove once bean flowers appear, to permit pollination.) Handpick and destroy adults and their yellow-orange eggs.

- **Holes in the leaves?** Look for the slender, pale yellow to reddish orange-and-black spotted bean leaf beetle, and handpick to get rid of them. Prevent damage with row cover until plants are ready to flower. Small holes in the leaves are likely flea beetles. Time planting earlier or later to keep the beetles from feeding on seedlings, or cover newly seeded areas with row cover.

- **Spotted, mottled, wrinkled, curled, or moldy leaves?** Problems like these are usually caused by fungal diseases, bacterial blights, or mosaic viruses. Prevent by planting resistant varieties, and keep garden clear of diseased debris.

- **Malformed or water-soaked spots on pods?** Suspect a fungal disease, bacterial blight, or mosaic virus. Prevent by planting resistant varieties, and keep garden clear of diseased debris.

- **Red spores or blisters on leaves or pods?** This is a sure sign of rust; catch this fungal disease early or rust can devastate your entire bean crop. Look for red spots on the underside of leaves or leaves that drop. Clip and dispose of infected leaves or pull up entire plants. Water only at ground level to avoid wetting leaves.

CHAPTER 5

BEETS

IF YOU PLAN TO COMPETE WITH BEETS, BE SURE TO PLANT plenty of them so you can enjoy all the tender leaves and roots before you carefully dig a few to take to the fair. If you think your beets can't compete in the beauty contest, you could still win a ribbon for your beet-growing efforts. Just look for the Creative Arts division in the show book, and bake those beets into something tasty, like a chocolate beet cake.

**AIT A SECOND.** Before you say, "I hate beets" and flip to the next chapter, consider that garden-grown beets bear no resemblance to the icky pickled beets some of us had to eat when we were growing up. Homegrown beets are just as sweet as winning a prize for growing them. Really.

Beets are also good for you. As a double-duty plant, all beet parts are edible — from the tips of the leafy greens to the tender roots. Some gardeners are known to plant an extra row of beets just to harvest and enjoy the tasty greens.

Beets belong to the goosefoot family (Chenopodiaceae). Swiss chard (sometimes called leaf beet) belongs to the same family.

People probably gathered the leafy greens for years before discovering the roots were edible, too. Food archaeologists believe the beets we plant and grow today came from *Beta vulgaris* subspecies *maritima*, the perennial sea beet that grows wild along the Mediterranean coast.

Experts say the Greeks were some of the first to cultivate beets for their greens centuries ago. They may have been responsible for naming the plant because beet seeds were thought to bear a slight resemblance to *beta*, the second letter of the Greek alphabet. Early Romans discovered medicinal uses for the roots. In the 1500s Europeans cultivated beets, probably the familiar red beets — the kind that bleed when sliced and diced. It wasn't until the 1800s when other colors of beets worked their way onto the pages of seed catalogs.

Now gardeners can grow many kinds of beets, in colors that range from deep magenta to gold or white. There are globe-shaped roots, long cylindrical roots, carrot-shaped roots, roots that are flattened, and perfectly smooth roots.

ROOTS MATTER

Whether the vegetable competition you're entering lists them as garden beets or table beets, the goal is to grow a plate of beautifully matched, blemish-free beauties. These beets are distinctly different from their cousins the sugar beet (used commercially to make sugar) and stock beets (called mangels or mangolds) grown as fodder for livestock.

If you want to win a prize for perfect, high-quality beets, it's good to remember that British gardeners refer to them by their old-fashioned moniker: beetroot. When planting this easy-to-grow root crop, the emphasis is placed squarely on the *root*.

Gardeners typically grow this vegetable as an annual, but the beet itself is a biennial plant. It sets its rosette of leaves and taproot the first year and then grows its flower stalk the next.

Some environmental stressors, like early and extended cool temperatures, can disrupt the two-year growth cycle and cause beets to bolt (form a flower stalk) prematurely in the first season.

When shopping for seeds, read catalog descriptions carefully. Some beets are grown more for their tasty greens than for their roots, so make sure the varieties you choose feature the roots as the main attraction. Look for beet characteristics that include smooth skin, attractive and uniform shape, improved germination, disease resistance, adaptability to a range of soils, high sugar content, and a long harvest period.

When looking at beet seed descriptions, you may notice choices such as organic seeds, untreated seeds, or treated seeds. Gardeners often opt for treated seeds to avoid problems due to soilborne pathogens. Other gardeners prefer to plant organic or untreated seeds. It's good to have options.

A BEET ABOUT GROWING

Because table beets aren't as sexy as other garden vegetables, contests offer fewer classes for exhibiting them. Contest rules will specify the number of beets to exhibit, their dimensions, and other display information, such as whether the tops should be trimmed and to what length and whether the taproot should be left intact or trimmed.

In addition to bolting, beets have other weather-related issues. Drenching rains that follow an especially dry period can result in roots with poor color. Long exposure to high temperatures while beets are maturing can

'Red Ace'

POTENTIAL PRIZEWINNING BEETS

ONE OF THE TOP BEETS FOR COMPETITION is 'Ruby Queen', a favorite among gardeners ever since All-America Selections added it to the vegetable winners list in 1957. Here are nine more beets that can also compete at the fair:

- 'Boro'
- 'Bull's Blood'
- 'Crosby Egyptian'
- 'Detroit Dark Red'
- 'Early Wonder'
- 'Merlin'
- 'Pacemaker III'
- 'Perfected Detroit'
- 'Red Ace'

CLASSIC ADVICE FOR SHOWING BEETS

IN 1909, THE RECOMMENDED long-rooted varieties of beets included 'Dobbie's New Purple', 'Pragnell's Exhibition', 'Sutton's Black', and 'Sutton's Dark Red'. The recommendations for exhibition were pretty much the same as today. *The English Vegetable Garden* (published that year) states that beets should be "of medium size, evenly tapering, regular, with a clean skin, and about twelve to fifteen inches long" with the young, fresh leaves left attached. But the tips for preparing the beets included soaking them for a half an hour in cold water before sponging carefully, and then removing any small rootlets with a sharp knife. The roots should be "syringed" just before leaving them to be judged. The exhibitors probably used a heavy-duty garden syringe to shower water or a secret solution over the roots to keep them fresh looking for judging.

cause zoning (the interior development of concentric white rings) and low sugar content. While zoning is valued in beet varieties like 'Chioggia', with its candy cane–striped interior, in others zoning indicates poor quality.

Something else to keep in mind about beets is their finished size depends on the variety planted and how much space the roots have to grow, not by maturity date. Once beets reach their full size, they're ready to harvest.

PREPARING THE SEEDBED

To grow superb beets, the ones contest judges are sure to relish, you need to give them a good start. For the biggest roots, plant beets where they'll get at least 6 hours of sun a day.

However, beets can take a little shade, especially in areas of high summer heat. When preparing the garden, consider the kind of soil that makes it easiest for beet seedlings to emerge. Remove weeds, rocks, soil clods, tree roots, and any other debris that can prevent beetroots from forming perfectly.

Avoid growing beets where beets, Swiss chard, or spinach crops grew the previous year. Rotating crops can help prevent fungal diseases. You can give beets a boost of soil fertility by planting where beans or peas grew the previous season.

Beets do best in loamy, well-drained soils that allow roots to grow uniformly and symmetrically. Even if you aren't trying to grow the longest beetroot, give your beet seeds the best possible start with a deeply cultivated (at least 18 inches), fluffy soil that allows seedlings to break through the top layer easily. Compacted soils will result in misshapen roots. One way to get deep, fluffy soil is by planting in raised beds. Some gardeners create deep planting holes in the soil by hammering in a tool like a broom handle. They fill the holes with a lightweight planting mix so the roots can grow completely unobstructed. If you don't have an ideal spot, you may be able to expand your planting options by growing beets in containers.

Beets grow best in soils with a neutral or slightly alkaline pH and grow poorly in acidic soils. Test your soil for boron to make sure there are adequate levels. Boron is an essential micronutrient for all plants, but especially for beets. Inadequate levels can result in beets that show internal black spot. (*Caution:* beets need only minute amounts of boron. Don't add boron unless you're sure the beet bed needs it; too much isn't good for plants either.)

Unless a soil test shows specific deficiencies, you can prepare the garden with compost, well-composted manure, or other organic matter and a balanced fertilizer. Dig in 2 to 4 inches of organic matter and work it into the top 6 to 8 inches of soil.

TIMING THE PLANTING

Plant beets in early spring, as soon as the garden soil has thawed enough for planting. Time your planting carefully for two reasons. First, as with growing anything for competition you want your beets to be ready for prime time at the fair. Also, with beets good timing can help you avoid some problems with insect pests and plant diseases.

Beets typically take 55 to 70 days to reach maturity, so stagger plantings and sow seed a week or so earlier and a week or two later. Beet seeds need cool soil to germinate, so where summers get hot be sure to plant before soil warms above 80°F.

SOWING BEET SEEDS

Beet seeds are different from other kinds of vegetable seeds. Each "seed" is actually a cluster of several seeds within a dried fruit, so several seedlings will sprout from a single seed ball, and they might show up at different times. If you want to eliminate thinning the multiple seedlings, look for monogerm beet seeds, which contain only one embryo.

Beet "seeds" are actually clusters of seeds that sprout in clumps; seedlings must be thinned to ½ inch apart (or more) to give roots enough space to develop properly.

Rinse or soak seeds in warm water for several hours right before planting to help speed germination. If you're growing golden beets, sow extra seeds to help ensure good germination.

Without compacting the soil where beets will be growing, drill shallow holes and plant seeds about ½ inch deep and about 1 inch apart in a single row, or in multiple rows 12 to 18 inches apart. Don't plant seeds too deeply or seedlings may have a tough time emerging.

Cover lightly with soil and gently water in with a light sprinkling. To keep the top layer of soil from crusting, making it difficult for seedlings to push through, cover the seedbed with row cloth or burlap, seal the edges, and use a hand sprinkler to water through the material. Seedlings will emerge in about a week.

It's a good idea to leave the lightweight cover cloth in place or stretch it over short hoops and seal the edges to give plants a healthy start and provide extra protection from pests.

THINNING THE SEEDLINGS

Because more than one seedling often emerges from a single seed ball, you'll need to thin at least twice if you want show-worthy beets. Without proper thinning you run the risk of harvesting no roots, or roots that are woody or misshapen.

When plants are about 2 inches tall, thin to leave only the sturdiest seedling in each cluster. Thin to about 1½ inches apart. Use small scissors or narrow-tipped pruners to clip seedlings at soil level, instead of pulling. Pulling can affect the delicate roots of the other seedlings. Rinse your thinnings and eat them in an early spring salad.

Thin again when beets are about 3 to 4 inches tall (1 to 2 inches in diameter) by digging up every other one. Leave at least 4 inches between plants so there's room for the remaining beets to grow. The small beets and greens are also good eating.

RECORD-SETTING BRITISH BEETROOT

GARDENERS IN THE UNITED KINGDOM have a special trick for growing extra-long beets for exhibition. They start with a cultivar such as 'Cylindra', prized for its ability to grow long, straight roots without twisting. They grow the beets in long drainpipes, suspended at an angle above ground and filled with a special homemade compost. A 2008 record for long beets was 21 feet long! As you can imagine, it consisted mostly of the long, skinny lower portion of the root with very little beet.

'Cylindra'

MAINTAINING THE BEET BED

While plants are forming their delicious greens aboveground, the beet is forming near the top of the soil, a long taproot with many smaller roots branching off it is snaking its way down through the soil as far as it can travel; the fleshy upper portion of this taproot is the beet. More than most garden vegetables, beets need consistent tender loving care all season so they can grow without interruption. The three essential gardening tasks are watering, weeding, and feeding:

Watering. Adequate water is critical to root growth, so keep soil moisture uniform by watering deeply and frequently, especially as temperatures start to warm. Drip irrigation works well for beets.

Fluctuations in soil moisture will cause slow development of leaves, cracked roots, hard or woody flesh, and poor yields. If under-watered, the leaves will start to yellow; if overwatered beet leaves turn darker and stop growing. Put simply, avoid soggy soil but never let soil or roots dry out.

Watch leaf growth because during the formation of the fifth and sixth leaves is when beets are most susceptible to stress. Sudden hot temperature changes and lack of moisture are especially problematic at this point. Either can increase ring formation in the roots (zoning), reduce sugar content, and cause bolting (going to seed).

After seeds have sprouted and soil starts to warm, add a thick layer of organic mulch to the seedbed. Mulch helps to regulate soil temperature and maintain soil moisture.

Weeding. Keep the area where beets are growing completely weed-free. Weeds provide a challenge for beets because they're competing for the same resources, especially space. Hand-pull weeds or use shallow cultivation to protect the beet's delicate roots from harm.

While you're weeding, cover up any beet shoulders that push up out of the soil to keep them from drying out. Beets with dry, cracked, or tough shoulders won't win any contests.

Feeding. If soil fertility is high at the beginning of the season, beets may not need any additional fertilizer. Just keep in mind low soil fertility can slow growth and result in poor-quality beets.

You can shoot for a moderate fertility level by giving beets a little nutrient boost about one month after planting and again at mid-season. Organic foliar sprays containing seaweed or kelp are an easy way to boost nutrients and promote healthy root development. Go easy on the nitrogen to prevent excessive top growth and poor-quality roots.

HARVESTING BEETS

Judges will be looking for beets with good color, good size, and smoothness of the skin

To keep from forming a tough core beets need fertile, evenly moist soil for steady, uninterrupted growth.

as well as a fresh, crisp interior. As the contest nears slice into a sample of beets to make sure you have high-quality beets to show.

There are two approaches to harvesting beets. Some competitors harvest them when beets reach the perfect size for exhibiting. Other gardeners wait until right before the contest to dig up their beets. Roots can remain in the ground for at least a week (possibly two) before their competitive quality starts to decline.

Use your hands to brush soil away from roots to see how big they are. Then use a garden fork to gently loosen soil next to the row and ease up roots, making sure to keep the thin root at the end attached. Work carefully to avoid damaging the thin skins on roots.

Clip long lengths of greens from beets before storing because they leach moisture from the root. Leave several inches of the stem attached, so you can retrim them right before the contest.

If harvested ahead of the contest, clean off soil, but wait to wash beets until right before the contest. Wrap each beet separately to prevent bruising and keep them refrigerated until it's time to prepare for the contest.

BEATING BEET PROBLEMS

Beets are known for being easy to grow, but you still need to be diligent. Keep your eyes peeled

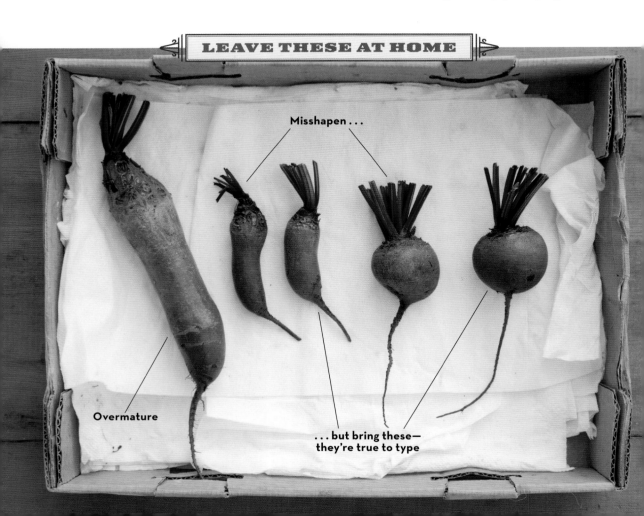

LEAVE THESE AT HOME

Misshapen . . .

Overmature

. . . but bring these—
they're true to type

for any pests or disease problems and take action right away. Here are some of the most common problems that can affect your beet crop.

- **Small pear-shaped pests underneath leaves?** These are aphids, which suck sap from the leaves, often making them curl. Prevent aphid damage by planting spring-blooming flowers near your vegetable garden to invite lady beetles and lacewings to feed on aphids or use row cover at planting time. If you do see aphids on your plants, dislodge with a strong stream of water.

- **Leaves stick together?** Look for green caterpillars with fine yellow and black strips; these are beet webworms. Crush the caterpillars and pick off damaged leaves. Search out and destroy eggs that hide on the underside of leaves. Keep beet bed free of weeds.

- **Seedlings disappear overnight?** Cutworms are to blame. Use cutworm collars to keep these pests away from seedlings.

- **Small holes in the beet leaves?** You've got flea beetles, tiny black insects that hop about when disturbed. Protect young plants with row cover, sealing edges well to keep out beetles. Flea beetles are less of a problem later in the season.

CHECKLIST FOR BLUE RIBBON BEETS

BEETS ARE TYPICALLY JUDGED in bunches of three to five roots. Harvest with the most tender, best-tasting beets in mind. Look for symmetrical, small to medium-sized beets (1½ to 3 inches in diameter) with narrow necks and smooth shoulders. Trim stems and leaves according to contest rules; check whether to clip or leave the lower portion of the taproot attached. Judges may slice beets to check the interior, so make sure the flesh is firm, crisp, and finely grained.

PICK
- ☐ Rounded, smooth beets free of side roots
- ☐ Small crown
- ☐ Uniform in color, size, and shape
- ☐ Tops trimmed according to rules
- ☐ Lower taproot intact, if required

PASS
- ☐ Beets with dry or green shoulders
- ☐ Misshapen roots
- ☐ Damaged, rough, streaked, or cracked skin

PRESENT
- ☐ Soak beets in water; use a soft cloth to gently remove soil
- ☐ Trim tops to specifications
- ☐ Remove any dry stems

A KID WHO CAN'T BE BEAT

JACY McALEXANDER

AT AGE 13, JACY McALEXANDER has just a few years' worth of vegetable contests under his belt, but he's already racked up an impressive list of awards at the Iowa State Fair 4-H Horticulture Competition. His champion cucumbers, kohlrabi, tomatoes, peppers, and chives have received recognition, but it's the 6-pound jumbo zucchini that tops his list of gardening accomplishments. How did he do it? "I just got lucky," he says. "I just let it grow."

It's not much of a stretch to say growing is what 4-H is all about. The national youth development organization helps kids cultivate life skills through a number of educational and hands-on projects. About 25 percent of young folks in Iowa are involved in 4-H, just like Jacy.

Jacy says he'd recommend 4-H to other kids because of all the activities and camps he gets to enjoy with his friends. "I'd tell them how much fun it is to work on projects, and how you learn about communication, leadership, and citizenship." One adventure included a trip to Minnesota, where

"YOU WANT TO HAVE ENOUGH SUN, BUT NOT TOO MUCH."

—JACY McALEXANDER

he spent the night in a museum, sleeping right beside dinosaurs.

Jacy entered his first vegetable competition a few years ago after he watched as his older sister, Brittany, competed as a 4-H member. It also helps that their dad, Earl, is a regional 4-H youth program specialist, and their mom, Kerrie, is involved as well.

While Jacy has been growing and showing for just a few years, he's been helping his dad in the garden since he was a kid. He plants in two different gardens, one at his house and one by his grandpa's farm. Of all the crops he plants, he likes growing hot peppers best. He'd like to try growing one of the superhot Ghost Chili ('Bhut Jolokia') peppers, if his dad lets him. He also has his sights set on winning the title of Pepper King one day. "That goes to the person who gets the most points for how their peppers were grown and prepared," he explains. "It would be really cool to do that, and you get a trophy, too."

Jacy enjoys gardening because he likes to watch things grow, especially when he's growing his own salads. He also appreciates the vegetable competition at the fair because it can be done all in one day. "We take them in, they judge them, and we find out the results at the end of the day."

As an accomplished young grower, Jacy is happy to share some of his gardening tips. For example, he says where you site your garden is important. "You want to have enough sun, but not too much, so you might need some shady spots." Also, some things need more water than others, and "you have to remember when to water," he adds.

"When it's time to harvest, you need to know where to cut the stem and how many vegetables you have to have on the plate" to meet the contest requirements. Jacy says "you have to try to pick things close to the same size, but it's hard to tell whether it will do well or not. You pick what looks like it isn't rotting." For those kinds of details, he refers to the 4-H publication that includes the rules, regulations, and information on what the vegetables are supposed to look like.

Horticulture is just one of the many 4-H projects that interest Jacy. He's involved with photography, robotics, home improvement, and community service projects, too. As a cancer survivor, he plans a community service project to raise funds for Children's Cancer Connections in Iowa. Together with a couple of his friends, Jacy has already sold more than 200 T-shirts as part of the nonprofit's Beat Cancer fundraising campaign.

GROWING FOR MAXIMUM WEIGHT

BRITISH GARDENERS COMPETE not only for records of beet length, but also for heavyweight records. In 2005 beet growers in Great Britain were shocked to hear a gardener in the Netherlands had grown a beet that was more than three times heavier than the existing record. They later breathed a collective sigh of relief to discover the ginormous 156-pound beet was an industrial sugar beet, not a domestic beet. Compared to that freak of nature, a 50-pound domestic beetroot seems kind of puny.

To grow a giant beet, use the best practices for growing a table beet, just with more of everything. For long beets you restrict the growth to a single long taproot. But for giants you want to grow as many bumpy, lumpy roots as possible. The more roots, the heavier it will be.

Some giant beet growers plant in aboveground barrels; others plant in raised beds. As with all giant vegetables, you want to start with beet seeds that have the genetic potential to grow really big.

Check rules to see if the contest is open to fodder beets (mangels), known for growing to mammoth proportions. Save any leftover mangels for brewing a batch of beetroot beer. I've read the high sugar content of the beets makes for an especially sweet and tasty ale.

TIPS FOR BIG BEET SUCCESS

- Plan for a long season, up to four months. Another option is to plant one year, let the root overwinter, and show it the next, if contest rules allow for it.
- Plant in fertile, deeply cultivated soil in spring. A good tip is to plant several times, over the course of a few weeks, to allow for poor weather.
- Plant seeds in groups of three, about ½ inch deep and 12 inches apart. Keep the soil moist after sowing seeds.
- Thin seedlings when they're about 2 inches tall, leaving the two strongest plants in each cluster.
- Check to see that roots are forming into small beets and then thin again; leave one plant about every 3 feet.
- Feed regularly with a balanced fertilizer; cover beet shoulders with soil as the roots form.
- Water deeply and frequently to keep roots from drying out or going to seed.
- Harvest carefully with a garden fork to preserve as many roots as possible.
- Clip greens right before the weigh-off to keep the root from losing weight on the way to the contest.

Fodder beets (which are called mangels or mangelwurzels in England) grow to mammoth proportions and often compete in a category separate from regular beets.

- **Tunnels inside leaves?** Tunnels are the work of the tiny larvae of leaf miners. Keep them from reaching leaves by installing row covers over young plants. Clip off and discard damaged leaves.

- **Small, light-centered circles on leaves?** Cercospora leaf spot is an airborne fungal disease that affects the greens, but may not harm the roots. Water at soil level to avoid wetting leaves. Clip off and dispose of spotted leaves.

- **Leaf margins that roll up?** Look for leaves that pucker along their veins and beet plants with stunted growth. All are symptoms of curly top virus, a problem spread by leafhoppers. Prevent the disease by using row cover and good weed control to keep leafhoppers out of the garden.

- **Seedling stems starting to weaken and collapse?** Damping off is caused by various fungi that are more problematic in weather that's too wet and cool or too hot and droughty. Replant seeds in well-drained soil; monitor soil moisture.

- **Yellow areas on beet greens?** These may be caused by downy mildew, which sometimes shows up on beet leaves as white or gray mold. Pick off diseased leaves and keep remaining foliage as dry as possible. If that doesn't slow the mildew, pull plants to keep it from spreading.

THE TALK OF THE TOWN

AMERICAN FOLKLORE HAS a rich history of "tall talk," especially when it comes to bragging about the quality of one's home-state vegetables. The boosters' club can give way to the liars' club, as in this 1851 example from folklore historian B. A. Botkin.

That year, the Commissioner of Patents reported an address delivered in San Francisco describing prizes for an onion weighing 21 pounds, a turnip "which equaled exactly in size the top of a flour barrel," another weighing 100 pounds, a cabbage measuring 13 feet 6 inches around, a beet weighing 63 pounds, and carrots 3 feet in length. Considering the entries in giant vegetable competitions today, most of this tall talk now seems like small talk.

CHAPTER 6

CABBAGE

GARDENING FOR COMPETITION ISN'T JUST ANOTHER DAY at the plant. It can be serious business, especially when you're growing cabbage. Whether you aim for perfectly round heads or a cabbage that weighs 100 pounds, you'll need good timing, plenty of pest protection, and tips from some of the best in the business. If you grow a great head of this cruciferous veg, you just might win some real cabbage at the fair.

YOU CAN FRY IT, steam it, ferment it, slow-cook it, and even roast it. But when you stir cabbage into soup, you're serving up a dish that's one of the oldest recipes around. Some experts believe people have cultivated this good-for-you vegetable for four thousand years, others say closer to seven thousand. But what's a few thousand years when describing this ancient edible? Nearly every country lays claim to a special recipe featuring some form of this cruciferous veg.

The cabbage family (Brassicaceae, also called the mustard family) is a big bunch, and cabbage is just one member of the clan. Cauliflower, broccoli, Brussels sprouts, kohlrabi, and rutabaga all descended from the same wild plants. Wild cabbages grew on the coastlines of western Europe, where people gathered them before they started collecting seeds and planting their own.

The common cabbage that found its way into early fields and gardens is a valuable part of our vegetable history. Whether green or red, round or pointy, smooth or crinkly leaved, cabbage deserves some special recognition. Long favored as "the medicine of the poor," cabbage's healthful benefits are now backed by research. One of its components, the phytonutrient sulforaphane, may reduce the risk of some cancers. Cabbage is loaded with beta carotene, vitamins C and K, and fiber.

It's also beautiful growing in fields and gardens. To me, cabbage's large leaves are just as attractive as the fancy-schmancy foliage of expensive ornamental flowers.

It's a shame more gardeners don't grow cabbage. Some lack the garden space; others may have tried but were frustrated by a season that ended with small heads, no heads, or a crop devoured by hungry cabbage loopers.

You *can* grow perfect heads of this old-fashioned vegetable. All it takes is selecting suitable types, timing the planting, practicing good cultural methods, and staying ahead of insect pests and diseases.

COMPETING WITH CABBAGE

For success with cabbage contests, start by selecting varieties that fit the head shape (round, flat round, conical, globe), color (green, blue-green, reddish purple), and leaf texture (smooth or crinkled) of the contests you want to enter. The show book will list classes such as round green, flat green, pointed green, red, as well as other kinds including Chinese cabbage and Savoy. There may be special jumbo cabbage contests, too. While you're checking the show book, make note of the schedule of the contest(s) you plan to enter.

Read seed and plant catalogs or search online for the cultivars that are known to grow well in your region. Note the number of days from transplanting until harvest, to help you plant at the right time for your contest.

For example, 'Late Flat Dutch' is a green cabbage that takes 90 to 100 days to mature. For a contest in late August, 'Late Flat Dutch' needs to be transplanted into the garden before the end of May. Because cabbage is a cool-season vegetable, and most vegetable contests are in late summer or early fall, the plants will be growing during the hottest part of summer. You may need to spread the planting dates over several weeks to give yourself more cabbage options. You may also need to harvest heads when they're ready and hold them in a cool place instead of leaving them in the garden to overripen.

CABBAGE THAT GOES KABOOM
Ever heard of exploding cabbages? For commercial cabbage growers, this bursting phenomenon

---

AT THE 2013 annual Giant Cabbage Weigh-Off at the Alaska State Fair, 10-year-old Keevan Dinkel competed against adults in the open class and won. Keevan, a member of the family famous for growing giant cabbages, won $2,000 with his 92.3-pounder he named Bob.

'TROPIC GIANT' FLAT

'LATE FLAT DUTCH'

'DEADON' RED SAVOY

'RUBY PERFECTION'

'MEGATON' ROUND

'FAMOSA' SAVOY

is as intense and forceful as it sounds. "The head itself is exploding to produce seed," explains Chris Gunter, vegetable production specialist and associate professor of horticultural science at North Carolina State University.

Because cabbage is a biennial crop, the first year is spent growing as a rosette and developing a head, storing the sugars and starches produced by means of photosynthesis. If left in the ground to overwinter, in all but the coldest climates the outer leaves die back but the head and growing point inside are protected. During the second year, the plant's new growth produces flowers that can develop cabbage seeds.

"In the botanical sense, a cabbage is a swollen terminal bud," Chris explains. If you look into the center of a cabbage at the microscopic level, you'll see its leaves and then its flowers. "If you dissect it, you'll see microscopic leaves until it undergoes a physiological switch, and instead of leaves it produces flowers right at the top of the core of the cabbage."

The goal is to encourage the formation of heads but not seeds, to keep cabbage from flipping that physiological switch. To switch from growing a leafy head to producing a flower, the plant needs a trigger. That trigger is pulled when the growing plant is subjected to a cold treatment. Commercial growers understand this happens not only when cabbages are left in the field over winter but also if the plant undergoes a period of cold weather in its first year. "You can see that happen if cabbage is grown from transplants, and they're planted too early in spring and we get a cold snap. They won't form a head; instead they begin to produce flowers," Chris warns.

Once flower formation is triggered, "all the chemical energy is used by the plant to send up a flower stalk in the center, and it has to get out." After a cold period, the flower stalk shoots up and tears through, either rupturing or literally exploding the head. The cabbage bursts open and the flower stalk explodes through. Chris says, "the pressure in the cabbage causes it to physiologically blow up. Instead of exploding into flower, it's like a fist slowly punching its way straight through the cabbage leaves and ramming its way up through the leaves." When this intense reaction, called bolting, shows up

Cabbage plants that are exposed to cold weather early in the season are likely to flower instead of producing a head of cabbage.

'Stonehead'

'Famosa'

'Ruby Ball'

POTENTIAL PRIZEWINNING CABBAGES

POSSIBLE PRIZEWINNERS may be hiding in this list. Some have been around a long time; 'Early Jersey Wakefield' and 'Charleston Wakefield' are heirloom varieties that grow cone-shaped heads. 'Red Drumhead' is another heirloom cabbage. 'Gonzales' is a mini-cabbage; its compact heads are perfect for smaller families and smaller gardens.

GREEN-LEAVED

- 'Blue Lagoon'
- 'Charleston Wakefield'
- 'Cheers'
- 'Dynamo'*
- 'Early Jersey Wakefield'
- 'Gonzales'
- 'Late Flat Dutch'
- 'Stonehead'*

RED-LEAVED

- 'Red Drumhead'
- 'Red Express'
- 'Ruby Ball'*
- 'Ruby Perfection'
- 'Super Red 80'

SAVOY CABBAGE

- 'Chieftain'
- 'January King'
- 'Savoy Ace'*
- 'Savoy Express'*
- 'Savoy King'*

NAPA-TYPE CHINESE CABBAGE

- 'China Express'
- 'Minuet'
- 'Rubicon'
- 'Tenderheart'

MICHIHILI-TYPE CHINESE CABBAGE

- 'Green Rocket'
- 'Greenwich'
- 'Michihili'

Denotes an AAS award winner.

prematurely during a cabbage's first season, it signals a cruel and untimely end to any chance for a blue-ribbon winner.

GROWING GREAT CABBAGE

Timing counts with cabbage. Plants can bolt if planted too soon and subjected to an extended cold spell. They'll also split if too ripe. Careful timing can sometimes help you dodge insect invasions. Cabbage can handle light frost, so plan to set out transplants two to three weeks before the last expected frost date for your area.

Select a spot in the garden that gets sun at least 6 hours a day. Avoid planting where any brassica relatives grew the previous year to reduce insect and disease problems.

Be sure to test cabbage heads before harvesting them. If you squeeze one and it feels loose rather than solid, let it grow a bit more.

Testing soil pH really pays off when planting cabbage. The ideal soil pH range for cabbage is between 6.5 and 6.8 to grow high-quality heads and to help minimize some soil diseases. Add a well-balanced fertilizer before planting and amend the soil with plenty of organic matter. Till the garden bed deeply (about 15 inches) before planting.

Start seeds indoors or buy transplants. Acclimate plants gradually to outdoor conditions. Transplant when plants have five or six leaves and set transplants so their lowest leaves are at ground level. Give cabbage room to grow; allow 18 to 24 inches between plants. Water well after transplanting. As plants grow, keep soil moist; don't let soil dry out.

Several weeks after planting, side-dress the cabbage patch with a rich compost. Keep up with fertilizing through the season, especially as heads begin to form.

Cabbage heads may look ready to harvest before the time is right. Test your cabbage by gently squeezing to make sure each head is solid. If the head feels loose, let it continue to grow and perform the squeezing test every few days. When ready, cut the head at the base of the plant or leave the contest's required length of stem. Heads can keep for a week or more if wrapped in plastic and stored in the crisper section of the fridge.

GROWING AND SHOWING CHINESE CABBAGE

Chinese cabbage (*Brassica campestris*, Pekinensis Group) is more closely related to other members of the cabbage (mustard) family than to ordinary cabbage. With tall columnar heads of green leaves and bright white midribs, it looks different from European cabbage. It also has a completely different history.

Don Francois
harvests
cabbages for
competition at the
Iowa State Fair.

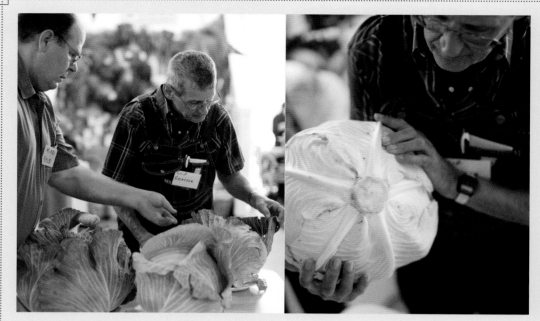

CHECKLIST FOR BLUE RIBBON EUROPEAN CABBAGES

CHECK THE SHOW BOOK for the number of heads you'll need to exhibit. If the rules require more than one specimen, your contest cabbages should match each other. Some fairs may also specify a weight requirement (such as 4 to 6 pounds) and the number of wrapper leaves. Contest rules may spell out the length of stem or whether you should leave the roots on the cabbages. Rules may differ slightly for green, red, and Savoy cabbages.

PICK
- ☐ Solid heads that are heavy for their size
- ☐ Wrapper leaves curl slightly at the edge
- ☐ Leave some stem to trim later
- ☐ Heads match in size, symmetry, and color (if more than one)

PASS
- ☐ Small, lightweight, or springy heads
- ☐ Heads with large midribs
- ☐ Yellow, wilted, or damaged leaves
- ☐ Insect damage or blemishes

PRESENT
- ☐ Leave two or three outer leaves (don't show a soccer ball)
- ☐ Wipe clean with a moist cloth
- ☐ Trim stem to specifications (usually ½ inch or less)

Chinese cabbage originated in the temperate areas of China, where it's been cultivated for about 1,500 years.

There are many kinds of Chinese cabbages. For competition you'll need either the heading (Napa) or the semi-heading (Michihili) kind. Napa types form tightly wrapped, barrel-shaped ("closed") heads. Michihili varieties are the tall, columnar ones with looser upright leaves.

Chinese cabbage may be a challenge to grow and show for a late-summer contest. These plants grow best in cool weather and make a better fall vegetable than one that needs to mature in time for August fairs. Gardeners can overcome this challenge by planting heat-tolerant (bolt-resistant) cultivars, planning for some partial shade, and maintaining consistent soil moisture. These babies simply can't be allowed to dry out.

The key to growing a winning entry of Chinese cabbage is the same as for any cabbage: steady growth. Plant in humus-rich soil, water consistently, and don't skimp on fertilizer. As with any cabbage, you can minimize problems by not growing where related plants were grown the previous year.

Michihili Chinese cabbage

Unlike the seeds of other cabbages, Chinese cabbage seeds can be sown outdoors as soon as the soil has warmed. Thin to 10 inches between plants when they're about 4 inches tall. Or you can start indoors, but sow seeds in biodegradable peat pots that can be planted in the soil. Using peat pots instead of bare-root

Napa Chinese cabbage

CHECKLIST FOR BLUE RIBBON CHINESE CABBAGE

DEPENDING ON THE CULTIVAR, an ideal head of Chinese cabbage is tall (12 to 16 inches) and wide (5 to 6 inches). Before harvesting, test Chinese cabbage for firmness by gently squeezing heads to make sure they're solid. Don't panic if some outer leaves are damaged, because those will be discarded anyway.

PICK
☐ Firm, well-developed heads
☐ Average to large size

PASS
☐ Immature or undeveloped heads
☐ Small or lightweight for the variety
☐ Yellow, wilted, blemished, or damaged leaves

PRESENT
☐ Remove roots and loose outer leaves
☐ Trim to a tight, cylindrical shape
☐ Cut stem cleanly at the base of the last wrapper leaf
☐ Rinse to remove any dirt

At fair time, when heads are firm and fully developed, harvest right before the contest by carefully uprooting the plant or cutting it from the roots. Keep cabbage cool and moist all the way to the fair.

PREVENTING CABBAGE PROBLEMS

Even if you maintain a healthy garden, there may be problems that can turn potential prize-winners into losers. Because different areas of the country have different problems with insect pests and plant diseases, check with your county's Cooperative Extension Service or local Master Gardeners to see what to watch for in your area. Here are the most common problems that can compromise a cabbage crop.

Cabbage root fly. It's an ugly scenario when the adult fly lays its eggs on the soil near plant stems. The worms (maggots) hatch and burrow into the roots of the plant, causing leaves to wilt and turn reddish purple. Prevent flies from laying eggs by placing cabbage collars on the soil around plant stems.

Cabbage worms and cabbage loopers. Those little white butterflies fluttering around the garden aren't so nice after all. They're cabbageworm butterflies, which lay eggs that grow into cabbage caterpillars that feed on foliage and can make a mess of a plant in no time. Cover young plants with row cover to prevent butterflies from laying eggs, and keep plants covered as they mature. Continue to search for worms by looking under leaves for the fat caterpillars. Pick by hand and drown in soapy water or destroy. While you're at it, pick off the cabbage loopers, too. Loopers look like green caterpillars with white racing stripes down their back and sides. They damage leaves and can ruin cabbages by eating their way through heads. Both cabbage worms and cabbage loopers can be controlled with the

transplants helps reduce bolting. Chinese cabbage requires less room to grow than round cabbage, only 8 to 12 inches between plants.

Mulch to keep weeds out of the garden. Avoid any deep cultivation, which may harm roots.

biological insecticide *Bacillus thuringiensis* (Bt). The easiest way to apply Bt is by shaking the dust over plants.

Alternaria leaf spot is a fungal disease that may develop on young plants. Aptly named, this disfiguring disease shows up as dark brown to black sooty spots on leaves. To prevent, use treated seeds and plant resistant cultivars, rotate cabbage-family crops, and refrain from overwatering. Using straw mulch around plants can also help.

Blackleg and blackrot are two bacterial diseases, and their names describe what happens to the plant's stem and taproot. They're just as bad as they sound. To dodge these diseases, select cultivars that resist black rot, look for treated cabbage seeds, and purchase only healthy-looking transplants. And the two principles of disease prevention are first, allow space for air to circulate and second, avoid overwatering.

Club root is a fungal disease that stunts growth, turns leaves a purplish color, and causes plants to wilt when the weather gets hot. Keep this from establishing in your garden by practicing crop rotation: avoid planting cabbage, broccoli, or cauliflower in the same place every year.

Fusarium wilt (yellows) is a common fungal disease that shows up as yellowing of the lower leaves of the cabbage plant and stunted overall growth. Avoid Fusarium wilt by planting varieties described as YR or yellows-tolerant.

DODGE DIFFICULTIES WITH THESE VARIETIES

Some cabbage cultivars have special properties that help prevent common cabbage issues. To head off problems, like lopsided cabbages that split and are prone to disease, try these:

Damage from cabbage loopers

Round heads: Cabbages that produce reliably uniform heads include 'King Cole', 'Savoy King', 'Cheers', and 'Megaton'.

Heat-resistant: Cabbages that grow well in hot weather include 'Ruby Ball', 'January King', and 'Stonehead' (also bursting tolerant); also 'Jade Pagoda' and 'Tenderheart' Chinese cabbages.

Split-resistant: Cabbages that resist splitting include 'Early Jersey Wakefield', 'Late Flat Dutch', 'Ruby Ball', and 'Parel'.

Disease-resistant: Plants known to resist some cabbage diseases include 'Caraflex', 'Super Red 80', and 'Blue Lagoon'.

BLUE RIBBON ◄ PROFILE ►

WHERE CABBAGE IS KING

ALASKA

WHEN SPECTATORS CROWD THE BLEACHERS at the annual Giant Cabbage Weigh-Off during the Alaska State Fair, they're hoping to watch a world record in the making. On the opposite side of the arena, the growers are hoping their season of hard work will pay off in a big way: in the size of their entries and in the thousands of dollars in prize money.

During the Weigh-Off — one of the fair's premier events — the spotlight shines brightly on cabbages that look like they should be growing next to Jack's proverbial giant beanstalk. These brassica behemoths have oversized leaves that can spread 6 feet wide with heads that can measure 2 feet across! The 2012 world record giant cabbage, grown by Scott Robb of Palmer, Alaska, weighed in at 138.25 pounds.

That record might not stand for long, especially when considering how big the champions have grown over time. At the fair's first weigh-off in 1941, the winning giant cabbage weighed 23 pounds. Max Sherrod, a local farmer, took home the $25 grand prize as well as lasting

fame because the fair's special giant cabbage contest for junior gardeners is named for him.

The growers in the Matanuska-Susitna (Mat-Su) Valley certainly have the advantage over gardeners in the lower 48. The Mat-Su, located about 35 miles north of Anchorage, is known as an agricultural hotbed for cool-weather crops.

"The real reason for our giant veggies are our long summer days. We have nearly 20 hours of sunlight per day in June," explains Stephen C. Brown. He's the University of Alaska Fairbanks Cooperative Extension Service agent for the Mat-Su and Copper River Districts, and a member of the board of directors for the Alaska State Fair.

Vegetables like cabbage may grow to XXL proportions because of the long days, but intense cultural manipulation has something to do with it, too. Stephen says cabbage competitors have spent years developing precise watering and fertilizing methods, as well as sophisticated systems for transporting their giants to the fair.

Growers work their horticultural hocus-pocus by developing their own hybrids, concocting fertilizer formulas, building windbreaks, and constructing shading devices to protect their cabbages from too much sun. Ask competitors for tips on growing giant cabbages and you might get some cheeky answers, like "fertilizing with Soylent Green" or giving credit to "the bicycle pump used to inflate them."

Unlike the hard-core competitors who hold their secrets like a winning poker hand, Robert Thom shares his growing methods with others. Robert is an experienced competitor who's entered his vegetables in fairs and exhibitions

for more than 40 years. He's collected many prizes over the years, but his biggest success was the 92-pound giant cabbage that captured second place one year. He's also grown a daikon radish that weighed 11.5 pounds.

Giant vegetables from his farm are well traveled, too. One year he sent a giant cabbage to Hawaii's annual 50th State Fair in Honolulu for a two-week exhibition that surely wowed the crowds. Hawaii hasn't been the only stop for Robert's giant produce. For several years he shipped big cabbages and other vegetables to Washington, D.C., where they were sliced and diced for U.S. Senate luncheons when Alaska Senator Ted Stevens was in office.

To grow giant heads of cabbage, gardeners need to start with the right seeds, Robert says. One of the main cultivars he's grown is 'OS Cross'. The OS stands for oversize, and this cultivar lives up to its name. It's a heat-resistant hybrid that produces enormous heads of cabbage that can weigh 70 pounds or more. 'OS Cross' is such a reliable performer, All-America Selections named it a vegetable winner in 1951.

For giant cabbage, Robert starts seeds indoors in March and transplants when the garden soil warms sufficiently in May. Cabbage may be a cool-season vegetable, but it prefers to get growing in warm soil. Robert advises planting as many as a dozen, so there will be at least one or two good ones to take to the fair.

When the fair rolls around in August, it's time to move the cabbages, which is no small feat. Cabbages, with all their leaves, need to be carefully harvested and quickly transported to the weigh-off because they lose weight with every passing minute. Competitors take extra care not to lose a single leaf, because each can add as much as 3 or 4 pounds to the total weight!

After arriving at the contest, volunteers wrangle cabbages on and off a special scale, all monitored by an official from the State of Alaska Division of Measurement Standards. As each weight is announced, the crowd reacts with appropriate oohs, aahs, and loud applause.

Depending on the number of entries at the weigh-off, and whether or not it was a good year for growing cabbage, there could be as much as half a ton of perfectly ripe cabbage ready for the kitchen. Now that's a slew of slaw!

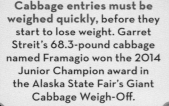

Cabbage entries must be weighed quickly, before they start to lose weight. Garret Streit's 68.3-pound cabbage named Framagio won the 2014 Junior Champion award in the Alaska State Fair's Giant Cabbage Weigh-Off.

THE GIANTS OF BONNIE PLANTS' CABBAGE PROGRAM

THE CHANCE TO BE PART OF something bigger than themselves is just one reason third-graders across the contiguous United States plant big cabbages every year. Since the Bonnie Plants Cabbage Program started in 2002, millions of kids have had the chance to get their hands dirty competing for scholarship money and the experience of growing a colossal head of cabbage.

Each year Bonnie Plants provides free 'OS Cross' cabbage seedlings to students who sign up for the program. The kids compete to grow the best cabbage (based on size and appearance) in their school class. Winners at the class level are entered in a statewide drawing to select one winner of a $1,000 scholarship from each state.

Bonnie Plants has a long history with cabbage. Now one of the leading providers of vegetable and herb plants in North America, the company was a small family operation in 1918. As beginning farmers, Livingston and Bonnie Paulk started selling cabbage plants to help make ends meet during the winter. They planted their first cabbage crop with 2 pounds of seeds.

Now the company gives away more than one million cabbage plants each year to help grow a crop of new gardeners. Kids, and their parents, get the chance to learn and grow together. For some of the participants, this is the first time they've ever tried their hand at gardening. Teachers get in on the action, too. Bonnie Plants provides classroom lesson plans to help support what kids learn in the garden.

Even though only one junior gardener gets the top prize in each state, every kid is a winner. Each cabbage that's planted and nurtured teaches valuable lessons about nature, responsibility, patience, and even disappointment. No doubt many kids will be inspired to continue gardening for a lifetime.

CHAPTER 7

CUCUMBERS

GROWING CUCUMBERS IS THE ORIGINAL DIY PROJECT.

Generations of gardeners have tried just about every growing method to get flawless fruit, from portable planting beds to complicated heating systems. But you don't need any special equipment to grow perfectly straight cucumbers. Just keep in mind cukes do best when the weather is hot and humid, and the soil is nice and moist.

CUCUMBERS WERE VALUED as a fruit from the very beginning, as long as three thousand years ago in the Himalayas. Just as today, the fruit was prized for its cooling properties and its high water content, which helped travelers stay hydrated on long trips. Cucumbers were also used to soothe insect bites, relieve sunburn, and aid digestion.

The temperate areas of central Asia may be where the long, sweet Asian cucumbers originated. It's likely the fruit reached Europe carried by invaders who traveled to Mongolia and brought seeds they collected along the way.

Spanish and Portuguese explorers brought cucumber seeds and pickles with them during their travels to the New World in the 1500s. Many sources credit Christopher Columbus with bringing cucumbers to Haiti for the sole purpose of pickling them.

A traditional recipe for pickling "cowcumbers greene" appears in the *Booke of Cookery*, the family cookbook Martha Custis Washington inherited in the 1700s. The pickle recipe advised soaking the cowcumbers in salted water for 24 hours, rinsing, and then storing them with dill in a less salty brine. It was important to keep the pickles in a covered earthen pot so "noe ayre come in."

> **IF YOU WANT TO GROW** the heaviest cucumber, try 'Mammoth Zeppelin'. These fruits can grow to 3 feet long and weigh more than 20 pounds! Going for the longest cuke? 'Telegraph Improved' can grow up to 8 feet long in a greenhouse.

COOL AS A CUKE

Cucumbers, whether grown on long trailing vines or on compact bushy plants, can take many forms. Cukes range from the familiar dark green, slightly tapered hybrid slicers to the short, blocky light green heirloom picklers.

Some have yellow-green peel and grow quite large while others stay small and round and pale. Some are spiny with deep ridges and others are smooth for perfect slicing. Most home gardeners grow their cucumbers outside, but special varieties including European seedless types are typically greenhouse-grown.

Gherkins, also called West Indian or Burr cucumbers, are a different species (*Cucumis anguria*). These small, spiny cucumbers originated in West Africa and were transported to Jamaica during the sixteenth century.

Vining cucumbers can be planted in vegetable beds or raised beds. But if you don't have the space for a tall trellis, you can plant bush-type cucumbers. The plants won't grow as tall as vining types — or produce as many cucumbers — but they can still win contests. Bush-type cucumbers will grow in a 5-gallon or larger container; a tomato cage works well as a support.

LEARN THE LINGO

A typical cucumber plant produces more male than female flowers, but it's the female flowers that set fruit. New developments in cucumber breeding include hybrids that produce plants with a higher proportion of female to male flowers, and plants that produce only female flowers. Here's a guide to help untangle the terminology when shopping for seeds and plants:

Monoecious: Plants that produce separate male and female flowers on the same plant.

Gynoecious: Plants that have almost all female flowers on the same plant. Gynoecious cucumber varieties need to be interplanted with monoecious cucumbers as pollinizer plants. Don't worry; seed companies mix in a certain percentage of pollinator seeds with the cucumber seeds.

'RAIDER'

'STRAIGHT EIGHT'

'MARKETER'

MEXICAN SOUR GHERKIN

'BURPEE PICKLER'

'JACKSON CLASSIC'

'BURPEE BURPLESS BEAUTY'

Hermaphrodite: Each flower contains both male and female parts, so they are self-fertile.

Parthenocarpic: Flowers produce seedless fruit without pollination. Parthenocarpic cucumbers are usually grown in greenhouses.

GROWING GREAT CUCUMBERS

Growing high-quality cucumbers is sometimes challenging because plants are susceptible to so many of the things gardeners despise: hungry insects, wilt, and molds. If you want to win ribbons for your cucumbers, plant in warm weather, protect young fruits from the dreaded cucumber beetle, train your plants to grow up, and keep an eye out for fungal diseases.

On the other hand, cucumbers can churn out quantity if not always quality. Once the weather warms, cucumbers can grow from seed to harvest in as little time as 50 days. Pickling cucumbers may peak even faster. Select cucumber types that are known to produce prolific crops of uniform fruit in your region.

Time your planting so you can either direct-sow seeds after the soil has warmed to 70°F. Or start seeds indoors in peat pots three to four weeks before transplanting. (If you plant pickling cucumbers, plant some dill, too. You'll be able to start pickling as soon as the first cucumbers are ready to harvest. In addition to exhibiting fresh cucumbers, you could enter the pickled products category, too!)

Plant in a full sun location, where cucumbers haven't grown in the last several years, to reduce exposure to soilborne diseases. Cucumbers like a loamy, slightly sandy soil that's rich in organic matter. A key to successful cucumber growing is to keep plants from drying out.

Cucumbers originated in hot, humid climates and that's where they grow best. If you live in a cooler clime and are serious about competing with cucumbers, you can try growing them in a greenhouse or a polytunnel.

It's important to grow cucumber vines up a trellis to keep them healthy and to grow straight fruits. Train vines to the trellis early on, when the seedlings are young.

TRELLIS TIME

To grow competition-quality fruit, you'll need to set up trellises prior to planting time. Trellised vines help grow straight, uniform fruit with even color with no yellow ground spots. Research shows gardeners get a higher yield from trellised cucumbers, too. Training vines to grow up helps keep vines safe, reduces the possibility of some disease and insect problems, and makes harvesting easier.

'Lemon'

'Marketmore 76'

'Suyo Long'

POTENTIAL PRIZEWINNING CUKES

MOST FAIRS OFFER TWO CLASSES of cucumbers: slicing and pickling. Because the cucumber has such a diverse nature, there may be additional classes such as dill cucumbers, English type (burpless), lemon, and gardener's choice. The bush types are good for smaller spaces; 'Bush Champion', 'Salad Bush', and 'Bushmaster' are good for growing in containers. Here are some top varieties for growing in your garden.

SLICING CUCUMBERS: VINING TYPES
- 'Cool Breeze'
- 'Marketmore 76'
- 'Slice Master'
- 'Straight Eight'
- 'Sweet Slice'
- 'Sweet Success'

SLICING CUCUMBERS: BUSH TYPES
- 'Bush Champion'
- 'Bushmaster'
- 'Patio Snacker'
- 'Salad Bush'
- 'Spacemaster'

PICKLERS
- 'County Fair'
- 'Diamant'
- 'National Pickling'
- 'Regal'
- 'Sassy'

UNUSUAL OR GARDENER'S CHOICE
- 'Armenian'
- 'Boothby's Blonde'
- 'Japanese Soyu Burpless'
- 'Miniature White'
- 'Silver Slicer'
- 'Suyo Long'

CHECKLIST FOR
BLUE RIBBON SLICING CUCUMBERS

SELECT CUCUMBER ENTRIES that are crisp, fresh, of medium size, and uniform in shape and color. You may want to slice open a sample to make sure the seeds are still soft. Cut fruit from plants, and take care to preserve the fruit's delicate skin from nicks and scratches. If you need to harvest a few days ahead of the contest, wrap cucumbers in plastic and refrigerate.

PICK
- ☐ Straight, symmetrical cucumbers 6 to 8 inches long
- ☐ Diameter matches contest specifications
- ☐ Uniform in color and size
- ☐ Unblemished skin

PASS
- ☐ Warts or corrugations on skin
- ☐ Oversized or misshapen
- ☐ Soft, overmature, yellowish skin

PRESENT
- ☐ Handle carefully to keep from damaging skin
- ☐ Remove soil with a soft cloth
- ☐ Trim stem to specified length

A good trellis for vining cucumbers is 5 to 6 feet tall, with a top and bottom brace and wire or plastic twine tied between the two braces at each plant. Other options include a wire teepee, fence, or lean-to. Bush types don't need such a tall trellis, but a shorter trellis or plant support will help promote perfect fruit. The goal is to keep vines off the ground and to allow fruit to hang freely, without touching anything that could scratch or damage tender skin.

Train plants to grow up or on the trellis by gently tying or using clips to secure vines to the trellis. To prevent spreading plant diseases, avoid working with plants while leaves are wet.

MAINTAINING

Install either row cover or individual plant covers to protect seeds and seedlings after planting. If cutworms are a problem, add collars to keep seedlings safe. Fertilize at planting with a balanced fertilizer such as diluted fish emulsion or manure tea. Mulch to reduce the need for weeding and to help maintain even soil moisture.

Cucumbers get their cool reputation because the fruit is about 95 percent water. Because of the high water content, plants will need consistent moisture the entire time they're growing. Water deeply to a depth of about 6 inches, especially while fruit is setting and developing. Try to keep the soil evenly moist but not soggy. To keep leaves dry, water at base of the plant and never on the leaves.

Fertilize one week after plants bloom and every few weeks through the season. Watch for pale or yellowing lower leaves, which may be a signal that plants need more nitrogen. Bronze leaves could mean plants are lacking potassium.

Though it seems counterintuitive, it helps to snip off the earliest flowers that form on vines. This cruel-to-be-kind method encourages plants to grow a healthier root system and more leaves before starting to set fruit, making for more cucumbers in the future.

TO PRUNE OR NOT TO PRUNE?

Some cucumber growers, especially those with small-space gardens, borrow pruning techniques from greenhouse growers to improve cucumber production and control growth. Pruning vining types of cucumbers to a single stem or leader directs energy to growing fruit instead of leaves. The technique is similar to pinching the suckers that form on tomato plants. Experts say pruning can increase yield and improve air circulation between plants.

Use your fingers, a sharp knife, pruning shears, or scissors to remove the lateral growth point (growth node) that sits between the leaf, the tendril, and the fruit. Make a clean cut as close to the main stem as you can without damaging it. Pinch or prune while it's still small. You'll also need to trim any new nodes that try to regrow at that point.

Some cucumber growers remove all lateral shoots on vining types. Others prefer to prune off only the first five or six lateral shoots near the base of the plant, or prune up to 4 feet and let the rest of the shoots grow.

HARVESTING

It's important to harvest cucumbers early and often. If you keep picking the fruits, the plants will keep producing. If you leave cucumbers on the vine too long, it signals the plant the end is near and the seeds should start maturing.

As the plant grows up the trellis, pick the cucumbers from the lowest part of the plant first and then work your way up to keep the top growth going. When plants are at their peak, you may need to pick cucumbers every few days; use a knife or pruning shears to make a clean cut from the plant.

It's best to cut cucumbers from their vines when they're still young and firm. Watch plants and snip off any cucumbers that are poorly shaped, too large, or turning yellow. These will be unsuitable for showing, and they'll slow other fruit production. Use these in the kitchen, or toss onto the compost pile.

If your cucumbers are headed to the fair, remove soil with a soft cloth but don't scrub off the natural bloom. This bloom is the powdery or waxy protective coating on the cucumber's skin.

WHY ARE MY CUKES CROOKED?

ONE OF THE MAJOR COMPLAINTS about cucumbers is fruit that doesn't grow uniformly straight but becomes misshapen with curling, crooks, or nobs. Blame environmental stressors like excessively hot or cold temperatures, low soil fertility, poor pollination, or lack of consistent soil moisture. All of these can affect fruit size, shape, taste, and overall quality. Cucumbers like heat and humidity, but too much can stress plants. Prevent sunscald or sunburn by encouraging a healthy leaf cover for fruit and keeping soil evenly moist.

You can work to eliminate the environmental stressors, or you can follow George Stephenson's lead. In the mid-1800s, he invented a cucumber straightener using long, slender tubes of glass to ensure perfectly straight fruit (see page 105).

PREVENTING CUCUMBER PROBLEMS

Most cucumber hybrids are bred to resist common plant diseases. You can avoid potential pitfalls by selecting cucumbers that have multiple disease resistance. Then keep a healthy garden by rotating cucumber crops, providing adequate plant spacing, maintaining good soil moisture (especially after fruit set), keeping leaves dry, and controlling weeds with mulch. Quickly remove plants if you spot an insect infestation or disease. Once vines start to wither, it's usually too late to do much to save them. Here are some common cucumber enemies and ways to cope with them:

Aphids are tiny pests that show up in clusters and cause damage by sucking sap from plants. Ants crawling on cucumber plants can signal aphids are near, because they're attracted to honeydew that aphids leave behind. A blast of water from the hose every few days will spray aphids away.

Cucumber beetles chew holes in leaves, runners, and young cucumbers. Delay planting in early spring to avoid the first rush of adults. Protect seedlings early in the season with row cover. Leave the row cover on until plants have grown and started to flower; then remove to allow for pollination. Prevent egg laying with a cover, like newspaper, spread over the soil. Handpick and destroy any of the black-striped or spotted yellow pests. Yellow sticky traps can reduce the need for this unpleasant task.

Squash vine borer (moth and caterpillar) likes cucumbers, too. Watch for the red-and-black adult, which looks more like a wasp or beetle than a moth. It usually appears in late May through late June. The moths lay eggs that

Spotted cucumber beetle

LESSONS FROM EARLY CUKE COMPETITORS

THROUGHOUT HISTORY, gardeners have devised intricate systems for extending the growing season for cucumbers, experimented with using different types of fresh manure in so-called hotbeds, and invented special equipment to produce flawless fruits. In *Vegetable Culture, a Primer for Amateurs, Cottagers, and Allotment-Holders*, Alexander Dean turned his attention to some of the practices used to encourage early ripening for cucumbers. "Originally it was the practice to grow these varieties in frames placed on manure beds, or else in brick pits heated by flues and hot manure," Dean related. He went on to explain that plan had fallen into disuse "because it is found to be so much easier to grow the plants in low houses heated by hot-water pipes, as in that way a suitable and equable temperature is easily maintained."

Dean's wasn't the final word on growing cucumbers. In his 1892 gardening guide *The Horticultural Exhibitors' Handbook,* William Williamson provided instructions for growing many kinds of vegetables for exhibition, including the English cucumber. These "are easily grown in a glass frame set on a hotbed," he said, although the best way to obtain "clean, straight, and handsome specimens" is by growing them in a properly constructed cucumber-house. This structure should be large enough for plants to be trained on wires near the roof, so "the cucumbers hang down from them, clear of all contact, and fully exposed to plenty of light and air." He also advocated the use of straightening

Cucumber straightener

aids, saying "fine specimens may be obtained with the aid of glass tubes to keep them straight and shapely."

Williamson's instructions included when and how to start seeds, how to plant in small hills, and how to maintain the hothouse at a humid and balmy 70°F at night. After three weeks, the fruit "should be thinned to a few of the most promising which are likely to be at their best on the date of the show." He advised gardeners to remove early cucumbers "to conserve the energies of the plant for the production of exhibition specimens." He also recommended frequent applications of liquid manure while cucumbers are "swelling."

grow into wormlike larvae that attack cucumber stems, causing sudden wilting of part of a vine. Protect with row cover, or plant cucumber cultivars that are resistant.

Pickleworm is a frequent nuisance to cucumbers and squash. Pickleworms are the larvae of night-flying moths that lay eggs on flowers and new shoots and buds. The young tunnel into buds, stalks, vines, and fruit. Use row covers to prevent moths from laying eggs, especially at night. Applications of Bt may help control larvae. Destroy infested vines.

Angular leaf spot is a bacterial disease that appears as angular or irregular shaped spots on leaves and fruit. This disease spreads rapidly by rain, hail, and contaminated equipment. Rotate crops, water at ground level to avoid wetting leaves, and avoid working or touching wet plants.

Bacterial wilt shows up as wilting and drying leaves before spreading to the vines. Remove and destroy sick plants. Control the cucumber beetles that spread the disease.

Downy mildew is an airborne fungus that shows up as yellow spots on the top of leaves and whitish patches of fungus underneath. Downy mildew is most likely to be a problem during cool, wet weather, so waiting to plant until warmer weather can help. Plant cultivars resistant to this fungus. Remove infected plants or use a fungicide at the first sign.

Powdery mildew shows up as round white spots on the underside of older leaves, especially during hot, dry weather. Eventually the

CHECKLIST FOR BLUE RIBBON PICKLING CUCUMBERS

THE BEST CUCUMBERS for competing in the pickling class are those specially developed to stay crisp through the brining process. Pickling cucumbers typically ripen faster than slicers, and the harvest can last only a week or two. Ideal picklers are about 6 inches long and less than 2½ inches in diameter. Select fruit that's straight or with as slight a curve as possible. Blunt ends are usually preferred to fruit with tapered ends.

PICK
- ☐ Straight cucumbers with spines
- ☐ Size meets contest requirements
- ☐ Cross-section is slightly triangular
- ☐ Unblemished skin

PASS
- ☐ Immature fruit
- ☐ Soft, overmature, yellowish skin
- ☐ Oversized or misshapen fruit

PRESENT
- ☐ Handle carefully to keep from damaging skin
- ☐ Remove soil, but leave the natural bloom
- ☐ Trim stem to specified length

fruits on infected vines will ripen prematurely and have poor flavor and texture. Give plants plenty of space for air to circulate, provide adequate water, and water at the base of plants to avoid getting leaves wet. Regularly remove dropped cucumber leaves from the soil surface.

Cucumber mosaic virus affects the quality of leaves, flowers, and fruit. New foliage shows up mottled or malformed. Prevent by planting disease-resistant cultivars. Treat aphids that spread the disease, keep beds weed-free, and immediately remove and destroy any infected plants.

SEX ᴀɴᴅ THE SINGLE CUCUMBER

If you've had meager cucumber crops in the past, it's likely plants aren't having enough sex in your garden. Most female cucumber flowers need pollen from male flowers to help them set fruit. But it isn't as easy as it sounds.

Early in the season, cucumbers may produce a dozen or more blooms, but these are usually all male — and they're the ones with the pollen. If the weather is rainy or cold, there may not be enough bees to help with pollination, and without pollination, female flowers can't produce fruit. This scenario typically results in slower and later production of fruit, and maybe even fewer cucumbers. Even if pollination happens, fruit that sets in cold weather may be malformed.

If you've noticed poor fruit set on the cucumbers, take pollination into your own hands. Start early in the morning when pollen is available. Locate freshly opened male and female flowers. Male flowers have short stems and pollen; female flowers have longer stems and a bulb or fruit shape at the base of the flower.

Clip off a male flower and remove the petals. Gently touch or roll the pollen from the male flower onto the stigma in the center of the female flower. Alternatively, you can leave the male flower on the vine and use a small paintbrush or cotton swab to transfer the pollen.

In addition to pollinating by hand, you can try to improve overall pollination in your garden by planting flowers that will attract more bees, like bee balm, black-eyed Susan, cosmos, sunflower, and zinnia. Another option is to select parthenocarpic varieties, which can set fruit without pollination.

Female cucumber flower

Male cucumber flower

CHAPTER 8

EGGPLANT

SO MANY EXCEPTIONAL EGGPLANTS, SO LITTLE TIME TO grow them. Even if you've never planted an eggplant before, you owe it to yourself to give it a try. These ornamental plants are prized around the globe for their good-looking fruits, which hide a delectable interior. Spend some time studying the list of potential prizewinners, and then plant several kinds to see which of your aubergines take home the ribbons.

EGGPLANT IS THE MOST EXOTIC of the mighty garden triumvirate that includes tomatoes and peppers. Meld these three ingredients together, and they make for some of the tastiest recipes on the planet. It's been that way for ages.

Some food historians believe eggplants originated in northwest India, where they've been cultivated for thousands of years. Others think the place of origin is China, where the early records of its cultivation appeared in 59 BCE. The eggplant also traveled west to Europe, where other cultures adopted this vegetable as their own.

If you visit India, Turkey, Greece, China, Egypt, Japan, Bangladesh, Malaysia, Indonesia, Spain, Italy, France, or many other countries, you'll find at least one national dish that features eggplant as the main ingredient. Notice any large North American country missing from the list? Eggplant is one of the least popular edibles in America. According to commercial eggplant producers, annual per-person consumption is about 1 pound of eggplant each year. In other countries, the per-person annual consumption can be over 100 pounds. Just let that eggplant fact marinate for a moment.

Because of its affiliation with its toxic cousins in the nightshade family (Solanaceae), eggplant wasn't widely accepted when it was first introduced to Europeans centuries ago. The fruit eventually gained popularity first in France in the 1600s, and then in England. Thomas Jefferson supposedly introduced eggplant to American gardens, but it took many more years before people started enjoying eggplant as an edible fruit instead of an ornamental.

There are several species of edible eggplants. These including the gilo (Brazilian *jiló*) or scarlet eggplant (*Solanum aethiopicum*), the Gboma or African eggplant (*Solanum macrocarpon*), and the most common garden-grown eggplant (*Solanum melongena*).

ALSO KNOWN AS EGGPLANT

If you don't like eggplant, you might enjoy aubergine, brinjal, melanzana, or a plate of "little dark blue things." How does that sound? The fruit that pops to mind when any American says "eggplant" has many different aliases around the world. Depending where on the globe you're standing, you might hear our ordinary eggplant called all sorts of names: garden egg, eggfruit, guinea squash, pea apple, king of vegetables, or brown jolly. Eggplant has also been called mad apple and the apple of insanity for its close association with other members of the nightshade family.

It seems the name is as well traveled as the fruit itself. Language experts say they can trace the etymology of *aubergine* to Sanskrit, the ancient language linked to India. The British named it egg plant, because the fruits introduced early on were small, white, and shaped like a chicken or goose egg. They gradually adopted the word *aubergine* from the French, which was derived from *alberginia* from Catalan, borrowed from something related in Portuguese, which in turn came from *al-bādhinjān* in Arabic, which was lifted from a similar Persian word, attributed to *vātin-gana-* (or *vātiñjana-*) found in Sanskrit.

The first aubergines exported from Europe to America were similar to the ornamental and edible variety 'Easter Egg'. Gardeners can still grow these small egglike fruits for an exceptional eggplant entry at the county fair. Americans are probably most familiar with eggplants of the large purple oval form. But there's a wide wonderful world of eggplants of every stripe such as long-fruited Asian types, teeny-tiny fruits, and others that look like an oversized drawstring purse. Every eggplant I've grown has offered nice velvety green foliage and lovely lavender flowers, and that's before setting its fabulous fruit.

'HANSEL'

'CLASSIC'

'BLACK BEAUTY'

'FENG YUAN'

'WHITE STAR'

To prevent damage to the fruits, grow plants in a tomato cage to keep them upright and off the soil. If individual eggplants touch the soil, place a leaf or other barrier under them.

Whether glossy globe or slender and slightly curved, the eggplants we grow today all began as small bitter fruits that took years to be tamed into something sleek and edible. Generations of seed-saving and crossbreeding made it possible for us to enjoy fruits that range in size from small eggs to large spheres in a range of rich colors.

COMPETING WITH EGGPLANTS

Most contests have several classes for eggplants: standard, Asian, and what I like to call "gardener's choice." Because there are usually only a few classes, spend some time reading through catalog descriptions. Maybe you'll decide to enter an eggplant in each category. Challenge yourself to show an exotic specimen the judges and fairgoers might not have seen before, like 'Applegreen', 'Turkish Italian Orange', 'Lao Purple Stripe', 'Thai Yellow Egg', or the enormous and impressive 'Rotonda Bianca Sfumata di Rosa'.

Whichever eggplants you choose, read the descriptions carefully. Match the number of days from transplanting to maturity to make sure you'll have a good crop, at the perfect stage, when the vegetable contests are accepting entries.

GROWING GREAT EGGPLANTS

Would it surprise you to learn eggplant is a perennial? The majority of North American gardeners grow eggplants as an annual because the climate isn't subtropical. But the plant can be perennial where summer nights are hot and steamy and it doesn't freeze in winter. Eggplants can be a bit temperamental to grow where conditions are less than ideal. They do best when they get what they want and can balk at any disruption to their environment. Cool weather, cold soil, hungry insects, dry spells, or anything that stresses the plant can hamper growth and production. However, if you're a conscientious caretaker, your gardening efforts will be rewarded.

In cooler climates you can set up water-filled plant protectors, plastic tunnels, or row covers to coddle eggplants. For perfect show-worthy specimens in the United Kingdom, gardeners typically grow their aubergines in greenhouses, using the same cultural practices and fertilizers as for greenhouse tomatoes.

Growing eggplants is similar to growing peppers and tomatoes (their cousins in the nightshade family). To grow exceptional eggplants, avoid planting in the same spot where they were planted during the previous two to three seasons. Also avoid planting where tomatoes, peppers, or potatoes grew.

Eggplants are adaptable to small-space gardens and can be planted in raised beds, square-foot gardens, and patio containers. Miniatures like purple-and-white-striped 'Fairy Tale' grow on plants less than 3 feet tall. Other good choices for smaller spaces include dark purple eggplants like 'Hansel', 'Patio Baby', and 'Ophelia'; white-skinned fruits like 'Gretel' or 'Ivory'.

TRY GRAFTED PLANTS

One way to grow better eggplants is to start with grafted plants. Commercial eggplant producers have used grafted eggplants since the 1960s to grow crops that are more tolerant of environmental stresses such as soilborne diseases, low temperatures, drought, and flooding. Growers who use grafted eggplants report fewer soil-borne disease problems, improved yields (50 percent or more), and plants that bear higher-quality fruit over a longer period of time.

Using a standard grafting technique, producers graft one eggplant scion onto another eggplant's rootstock. Growers typically use an eggplant that produces higher quality or

EARLY EGGPLANT EXHIBITIONS

EGGPLANT WASN'T ALWAYS INCLUDED in horticultural contests, at least in the British Isles. It was left out of the extensive exhibition list of the 1892 "Horticultural Exhibitors' Handbook" published in Scotland. One reason may be that eggplants were difficult to grow in cool climates, especially before the development of modern varieties. The bulletin "Exhibiting Fruit and Vegetables in British Columbia" (1913) explained that the "Egg-Plant" class was only in "the Dry Belt sections" of the province.

But culinary tastes may be the real reason. Edwin Beckett addressed the topic of eggplants (*Solanum esculentum*) in his 1899 gardening book *Vegetables for Exhibition and Home Consumption in the United Kingdom*. Winner of a gold medal for vegetables from the Royal Horticultural Society, he explained that eggplants had limited appeal as an edible among gardeners in the United Kingdom. In France and other "continental countries," he said they are largely cultivated for culinary purposes, and "when properly served they form a most acceptable dish to those who have acquired a taste for their handsome fruits." In England, eggplants were then usually cultivated for ornament only, and, as Beckett noted, "when grown and carrying a heavy crop of fruit, the plants present a highly attractive appearance." Although it wasn't fashionable to harvest the fruits, Beckett deigned to explain how gardeners and cottagers could present "egg plants" for the show bench, adding that "for exhibition, in a mixed collection of vegetables arranged for effect, these are very useful and always admired by the visitors."

'Classic' 'Ichiban' 'Nubia'

POTENTIAL PRIZEWINNING EGGPLANTS

HERE ARE SOME FAVORITES gardeners recommend taking to the show:

STANDARD
- 'Black Beauty'
- 'Black King'
- 'Classic'
- 'Prosperosa'

ASIAN
- 'Early Long Purple'
- 'Ichiban'
- 'Millionaire'
- 'Ping Tung Long'
- 'Purple Comet'

OTHER
- 'Casper'
- 'Early Black Egg'
- 'Nubia'
- 'Rosa Bianca'
- 'Thai Long Green'

better tasting fruit for the scion, grafting this onto a tougher, more disease-resistant rootstock. The rootstock typically is chosen for high resistance to soilborne diseases (Verticillium wilt and bacterial wilt), or soil-dwelling parasites like root-knot nematodes. Grafted eggplants can also thrive in less-than-ideal soil conditions.

You can now grow grafted eggplants, too. Investing in grafted eggplants could be helpful in small-space gardens that have soil problems or limited space for rotating crops every year. The important thing to remember when planting grafted eggplants is to make sure the graft union is above the soil line. This prevents the union from rooting in the soil, which would negate the benefits of using a grafted rootstock.

PLANTING

Eggplants are usually grown from transplants. They may take a long season, sometimes more than 80 days from transplanting until the first harvest. To time your seed-sowing, consider your region's last average day for spring frost, but also allow time for nighttime temperatures to warm considerably before planting. Eggplants like hot weather, but during exceptionally hot days the flowers may not set fruit. Where summers are hot, time planting carefully so fruit will set before temperatures heat up in your garden.

Start seeds indoors 8 to 10 weeks before transplanting outdoors. Baby them with bottom heat to help with germination. After they show a few leaves, transplant into individual pots and place them under grow lights to keep them warm.

Another option is to wait until frost is a distant memory and purchase healthy transplants from a garden center known for providing high-quality care to their plants. With eggplants, problems that start early can last all season.

Acclimate plants adequately before planting outdoors to reduce transplant shock and to give roots a good start. Wait for warm soil (above 60°F) and warm nights (55°F) before planting because cold roots and cool nights will slow their early growth. Cold weather can also cause misshapen or poor quality fruit.

Researchers who study eggplant production say it's better to transplant into larger containers if necessary, than to plant them in the garden while the soil temperatures are still cool. If you're in a hurry to get planting, use black plastic mulch to warm the soil. When soil and plants are ready, cut holes in the plastic and plant.

Choose a spot in full sun, in fertile, well-drained soil for your transplants. Give eggplants plenty of room to grow by spacing them 18 to 24 inches apart, with 3 feet between rows. Try not to disturb plant roots once they're in the ground.

Think optimistically and plan ahead. Add a tomato cage or other support to prevent branches from breaking under heavy fruit loads. Supports are especially helpful to keep fruit off the ground and for growing straighter Asian eggplant varieties. The cage also makes it easy to quickly cover the plants during an unexpected cold snap, or to protect the plants from damaging winds.

MAINTAINING

Eggplants grow best with consistent deep watering. Where rainfall is scant, you'll need to supply several gallons of water for each plant, each week. Drip irrigation is a good method for keeping foliage dry while maintaining soil moisture when fruits are forming and growing.

Uneven soil moisture can show up as blossom-end rot or poorly formed fruit. If leaves yellow, show spots, and start to drop, it could signal a water deficit; too much water will show up as flowers that drop without setting fruit. Blossoms may also drop during extreme temperature fluctuations.

Eggplants need a constant supply of nutrients during their growing season. Feed with a

Double-fruited eggplants won't win in regular competition, but you can enter them in the novelty category.

Simply entering a less common variety, such as 'White Star', can increase your odds of taking home a ribbon.

To test an eggplant for maturity, gently press the skin with the pad of your thumb. If the indentation springs back to normal, it's ripe. If the indentation remains in the skin, it's not ready for the fair.

BEE KIND TO YOUR EGGPLANTS

TO GROW A GOOD CROP of eggplants, you'll need to get buzzing. Bees are the primary pollinators of eggplant flowers, and bumblebees do most of the heavy lifting. Buzz pollination happens when a bumblebee lands on a flower and gives it a big hug to force out the pollen. To create this kind of activity, you'll want to attract as many bumblebees as you can to your garden. Here's how to provide what bees need:

- Select suitable flowering plants rich in nectar and pollen, such as borage, bee balm, lavender, sunflowers, black-eyed Susan, blanket flower, lupine, cotoneaster, sage, aster, and mints.
- Choose a variety of flower colors (especially blue and violet), shapes, and scents.
- Plant clumps of three or more of each kind of flower.
- Look for flowers that bloom over a long period.
- Overlap bloom times, from early spring into late fall, so something is always in flower.
- Mix in native wildflowers that are adapted to your region's climate and soil.
- Avoid plants with showy double and triple flowers; their pollen is hard to reach.
- Provide a source of clean water like a birdbath, a water garden, or a shallow dish.
- Avoid using insecticides in the garden, or use the least toxic type and spray at night when bees aren't active.

balanced liquid fertilizer when plants have set a few fruits. Plants may need an additional boost of fertilizer every few weeks during the season to promote growth and fruit production.

Add thick layers of organic mulch to help maintain soil moisture and reduce the need for cultivation. If weeds appear, hand pull or use shallow cultivation to avoid damaging plant roots.

HARVESTING

A common mistake for beginning growers is waiting to harvest the eggplants until they're as large as those found in grocery stores. If fruit is left too long, the production of fruit will slow or stop, and the fruit that remains on the plant will lose its sheen and become seedy.

Keep track of the average days to harvest for each eggplant, and start checking fruit around the estimated maturity date. Another indicator is size; watch to see when eggplants reach their estimated mature size.

Even if you're still well in advance of the contest, start harvesting and eating as soon as eggplants are ready. Picking will result in a higher yield overall. Use pruners to carefully clip fruit from the stem to avoid damage. Eggplants bruise easily, so handle with care by putting the emphasis on *egg*. Fruit quality can decline quickly; refrigerate for one or two days at the most. Commercial eggplant producers hold eggplants at a temperature of 45 to 50°F and 90 to 95 percent relative humidity.

PREVENTING PROBLEMS

Eggplants are susceptible to the same insect pests and disease problems of related tomatoes, peppers, and potatoes. You can avoid most problems with good cultural practices. Keep the garden clear of plant debris and weeds, make sure there's good drainage, plant healthy transplants, and maintain good soil fertility.

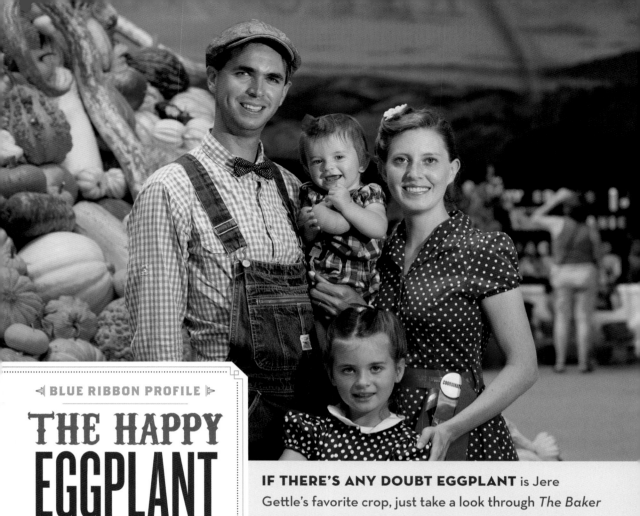

THE HAPPY EGGPLANT HUNTER

JERE GETTLE

IF THERE'S ANY DOUBT EGGPLANT is Jere Gettle's favorite crop, just take a look through *The Baker Creek Vegan Cookbook*. Its recipes from the Gettle family kitchen include Heirloom Roasted Eggplant Pizza, Baba Ghanoush, Breaded Heirloom Eggplant Cutlets, Russian Eggplant-and-Shiitake Pockets, and Ping Tung Eggplant Cake.

Gettle, the founder and owner of Baker Creek Heirloom Seeds in Mansfield, Missouri, loves the eggplant for its culinary uses. "I love to eat it because there's a lot of variation in the flavor, depending on the variety." He eats a lot, too: "I eat 100 to 150 pounds of eggplant a year," he says. "In the summer I eat it maybe two or three times a day, in some form or another."

Exploring for Eggplants

Jere also likes to collect eggplants. Every year he plants more than 70 different varieties, and he appreciates every single plant. "They're easy to grow and they have beautiful flowers and foliage, too."

He credits his expanded vision of eggplant to a trip to Thailand in 2002. That's when he had the chance to see what an important food crop it is to people in other places of the world. It was exciting to walk through open-air marketplaces, filled with vendors and shoppers in their native dress, and see more than 20 different varieties of eggplant for sale. In places like Thailand — and India, Indonesia, Korea, and Japan — eggplant is served raw in salad bars, steamed, baked, pickled, jellied, blended into chutneys, and made into candies and sweet cakes.

While eggplant hunting, Jere searches for the most interesting varieties to bring home and share with other gardeners. Once he finds a unique variety, like 'Thai Lavender Frog Egg', he'll look for a ripe eggplant hidden somewhere in the pile. "That can be difficult, because most of the fruit is sold in the immature stage, when it tastes the best," he explains. "But usually I can find a couple of overripe ones to buy and then scrape out the seeds."

If the seeds germinate, they'll be planted in the company's Missouri trial gardens. Then, if the plants and fruit meet Baker Creek's exacting standards, the eggplant could be featured in the seed catalog. That might happen right away, or it might take years. It all depends on what other projects (and eggplants) Jere has on his plate.

Choice Varieties

One of his many favorites is 'Malaysian Dark Red'. This variety appeals to him because of its dark reddish skin, which is matte with a parchment-like finish, instead of shiny. The eggplant grows to about 10 inches long and tastes "tremendous."

'Rosita', from Puerto Rico, is another of Jere's top choices. The fruit of this plant is bright neon purple with pink undertones, and its flavor is especially appealing to those who prefer bitter-free fruit.

Jere says the most popular eggplant in the Baker Creek catalog is 'Aswad', the seeds of which were sent to him from a friend in Iraq. The fruits are big and blocky and grow to weigh 3 pounds or more.

Tips from an Eggplant Enthusiast

For success in eggplant growing, Jere recommends giving plants a medium-rich soil, just like that for tomatoes and peppers. It's especially important to remember eggplant originated in a climate with warm nights. "It's better to wait and put them out the first of June instead of the first of May," he says. "They'll grow just as fast or faster, and they'll make (form) really quick."

Another tip is to treat plants for flea beetles as soon as they're transplanted. Jere recommends spreading diatomaceous earth on the leaves of plants to repel the harmful pests. Sprinkle the powder on the foliage after a rain, and re-treat plants several times a week until the flea beetle invasion is over.

Jere says it would be difficult for him to judge eggplant entries at a vegetable contest, because he'd be most interested in only one thing: flavor. "There's so much to consider," he adds. He's never satisfied, because "there are always new eggplants to try, something new on the horizon." He also says if he had to choose only one crop to grow, it would probably be eggplant. "It always takes up more room in the garden than it should."

'Rosita' eggplants

CHECKLIST FOR BLUE RIBBON EGGPLANTS

LOOK FOR FRUITS that are medium to large and firm, with a uniform, deep color and glossy sheen. To make sure eggplants are ready to exhibit, apply the thumbprint test. Lightly press your thumb into the eggplant. If the pressure leaves a dent, the eggplant is not ripe and shouldn't be harvested. If the thumbprint springs back it's ready to be picked.

Harvest eggplant as close to the competition as possible, so the "cap" or calyx is fresh and green, with no brown edges. Use hand pruners, scissors, or a knife to cut fruit from the plant. Cut into a sample fruit to make sure seeds are still soft; hard seeds mean an eggplant is overmature. Exhibiting younger fruit at the fair is better than showing specimens that are past their prime. Handle carefully to prevent bruising or dulling the skin with oily fingerprints.

PICK
- ☐ Heavy, firm, shiny eggplant
- ☐ Uniform color
- ☐ Small blossom scar
- ☐ Cap and stem still attached
- ☐ Unblemished skin

PASS
- ☐ Undersized or overmature with hard seeds
- ☐ Dull skin or off-color for the type
- ☐ Bruises, dark spots, blemishes, or damage
- ☐ Dry, brown cap

PRESENT
- ☐ Handle with care to prevent bruising
- ☐ Gently wipe with a damp cloth; don't scrub or polish; trim stem to specifications (usually 1 inch beyond calyx base)

Rotating crops helps prevent soilborne diseases and also reduces depletion of soil nutrients. Aim for growing big plants with good leaf cover to protect fruit from sunscald (a plant's version of sunburn, which shows up as pale spots on fruits). In addition to the problems described under tomatoes and peppers, here are a few that may crop up:

Colorado potato beetles are yellow-and-black–striped pests that harm potato crops and are also damaging to eggplant, peppers, and tomatoes. These beetles are eggplant enemies because they devour leaves and ruin entire crops. Check plants daily for the pests and handpick.

Spider mite infestations can show up as small specks on leaves before the leaves turn yellow and drop. Spider mites can cause a plant to quit producing. Check the underside of leaves for the small red mites, and use high-pressure water from the hose to knock them off.

Flea beetles can make leaves look like they've been hit with buckshot, so they must be stopped before they can get started. Exclude flea beetles by covering plants with row cover cloth sealed at the edges, or cover individual plants until flowering begins.

Cutworms like tender eggplant transplants and can take down a young transplant overnight. Keep them away by placing collars around the stems at planting time.

Verticillium wilt is a soilborne disease that starts in the roots and can result in little or no fruit. If plant leaves suddenly wilt and turn brown, this may be the culprit. You can prevent problems with wilt diseases by rotating crops, but avoiding rotations among tomatoes, peppers, potatoes, and eggplant.

LEAVE THESE AT HOME

Scarred

Overmature

Not glossy enough

Insect damaged

Cracked

CHAPTER 9

ONIONS

EVEN IF YOU DON'T WANT TO GROW AN 18-POUND ONION, you probably want to grow a perfect one. Two keys to growing great globes are selecting onion cultivars that will get the right amount of daylight in your garden and then giving your onion crop plenty of fine fertilizing. No matter which varieties of onions you decide to plant, growing healthy leaves is the most important task and the one that helps distinguish the winners.

THE AVERAGE AMERICAN eats at least 20 pounds of onions every year without giving it a second thought. It's such a simple act to write *onions* on the grocery list, grab a few pounds, take them home, and then start chopping. But what if we never had the chance to relish the sweet, mild, or wild taste of these breathtaking orbs?

Home cooks, hash slingers, snooty foodies, and famous chefs can all agree the onion is irreplaceable. Even Julia Child is quoted as saying "It's hard to imagine civilization without onions." They're an essential ingredient for just about every savory recipe created.

The ordinary onion may have originated as long as five thousand years ago, probably near the Mediterranean. Other alliums may have started out in Asia. The ancient Egyptians grew onions, as did the early Greeks and Romans. Onions became a staple in Europe because they were one of the few foods that could be stored without spoiling, although those first onions were nothing like the good-looking globes we grow today. We owe the onion's uniformity to seed savers and hybridizers who worked for years to develop onions that are consistent in size, shape, color, and overall quality.

In 1909 the experts writing *The English Vegetable Garden* made it a point to recognize the advances seen in onions at vegetable exhibitions over the years. "Few vegetables, especially from an exhibition point of view, have been more improved during the last few years than the Onion," they reported. "It now forms one of the most important and interesting subjects at all our vegetable exhibitions, and no collection of vegetables at any season of the year is complete unless a dish is included." Consequently, they advised, "all interested in the production of high-class vegetables must endeavor to produce the finest specimens. Fortunately Onions are not fastidious as to soil or position. Anyone with a garden and who is prepared to take the necessary trouble can excel in their culture."

NO POSIES, PLEASE

ONIONS ARE BIENNIAL: they take two years to grow and seed. Onion growers tinker with this process, using temperature and/or transplanting to produce onion seeds.

However, these same methods can work against gardeners who want to grow flawless onions for competition. When onion plants are subjected to fluctuating cold and warm temperatures, their growth fluctuates, too. These temperature swings tell plants to go dormant and then start growing again, as if they'd already reached their second year. This roller-coaster ride causes onion bulbs to flower prematurely. Once a plant sends up a flower stalk, it's still edible — but it won't win any prizes.

Prevent premature flowering (bolting) by selecting onion varieties matched to your region and planting at the recommended time. Plant onion transplants that are pencil-sized or smaller in diameter. Minimize stress on plants with proper cultivation and care.

While most onions are biennial, gardeners can grow perennial types, too. Egyptian or walking onions (*Allium cepa*, Proliferum Group) are hardy onions that grow bulblets (bulbils) at the top of their leaf stalks. When the bulblets fall, they plant themselves where they land. This "walking" through the garden means they'll grow new leaves and topsets each year. These onions go by other names such as topsetting winter onions (because they overwinter well), tree onions, or top onions.

During the 1800s in the United Kingdom, nurserymen such as William Robinson worked to improve the quality and size of onions by collecting seeds from only their best specimens. After he started winning prizes at

'HIGHLANDER'

'SUPER STAR'

'RED RIVER'

local vegetable exhibitions, Robinson began marketing seeds under the Mammoth trade name. That tradition continues today at W. Robinson & Son Seeds and Plants in England. Its line of Mammoth onions, leeks, beets, cucumbers, marrows, cabbages, pumpkins, and peas are bred especially for the "show bench."

WHAT IS AN ONION, ANYWAY?

An onion isn't a fruit or an ordinary root. It's a vegetable that's made up of many layers, but dig deeper and you'll see those layers are just a bunch of leaf bases. If you want to grow and show the biggest and best onions, it makes sense to do everything possible to grow plants that have a lot of healthy leaves.

One of the ways to start leaf-building is to plant your onions early enough so there's plenty of top growth before the bulb begins to form. Onions are a cool-season biennial vegetable that can be planted three ways: as seeds, sets, or transplants.

Marty Schnicker's giant onion

Onion seeds are collected from dried onion seed heads and are quite small. Seeds can be directly sown in the garden in areas with long and warm growing seasons. Elsewhere, they need to be started indoors 8 to 10 weeks before the average last frost date. Seeds give you the most options for choosing varieties, but it takes time and patience to grow from seeds.

An onion set is a small bulb that will grow into a larger bulb; it's already gone through one bulbing process. Sets produce bulbs faster than starting from seeds, but you won't have as large a selection of different varieties. Also sets have the potential for carrying plant diseases. Plant onion sets early in spring, four to six weeks before the last frost date and just as soon as the garden soil is workable.

An onion transplant is a small onion plant, usually 8 to 10 weeks old, that hasn't formed a bulb, but will if planted at the right time, which is early spring. Transplants already have several leaves and give you a head start on the growing season, but you need to get them in the ground as quickly as possible, even if it means planting in cold, wet weather.

When you plant seeds, the promise of a successful crop starts when the first leaf breaks through the surface of the soil. That leaf looks like a thin green loop at this stage. As the next leaf appears, the loop begins to stand up, looking like a flag blowing in the wind.

As more leaves appear, the first leaf dries up. More leaves appear, and the neck of the onion starts to thicken like an expanding vase holding a growing number of leaves. Leaves continue to appear until bulbing begins just beneath the surface of the soil.

The number of healthy leaves is a good indicator for how big the finished bulb will be. Medium-sized onions have around 9 leaves, large onions about 13, and giant-onion growers strive for 20 or more big leaves.

POTENTIAL PRIZEWINNING ONIONS

EVEN IF YOU CAN'T GROW JUMBO ONIONS, you'll still have a chance at a ribbon by showing smaller, equally perfect onions. Here are the top onion recommendations for each of the most popular contest classes:

SHORT-DAY ONIONS
- 'Giant Red Hamburger'
- 'Texas Early Grano'
- 'Texas Supersweet 1015Y'
- 'Yellow Granex Hybrid'

INTERMEDIATE-DAY ONIONS
- 'Candy'
- 'Red River'
- 'Super Star'

LONG-DAY ONIONS
- 'Copra'
- 'Cortland'
- 'Red Wethersfield'
- 'Valencia'
- 'Walla Walla'

GREEN OR BUNCHING ONIONS
- 'Evergreen Hardy White'
- 'Tokyo Long White'
- 'White Lisbon'
- 'White Spear'

'Red River'

'Super Star' IOWA STATE

The bulb continues to grow as leaves bend and fall away. Without leaves for support, the neck begins to soften and the remaining leaves fall over. These fallen leaves are the signal the bulb is ready to harvest.

HOW TO SELECT VARIETIES

Onions for exhibition typically include round or flat dry onions (red, white, and yellow), green bunching onions, and small pickling onions. Some events may also include leeks, shallots, and garlic in separate classes, and there also may be contests for jumbo or giant onions.

For the best onion growing success, match onion selections to the area of the country where you plant your garden. Any of the dry onions you'll grow are inherently smart. They know it's time to start forming bulbs when the number of daylight hours (or day length) meets their precise requirements. Onion varieties are described as short-day, intermediate-day, or long-day to help you pick the right one for your region.

ADVICE FROM THE ONIONMAN

BRUCE FRASIER

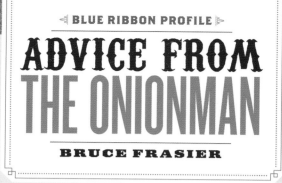

IF YOU'RE WORRYING about the onion transplants you spent all afternoon planting, multiply that amount of worry by 900 million. That's the number of onion plants Bruce "Onionman" Frasier frets about every season. As president of Dixondale Farms in Carrizo Springs, Texas, Bruce is in charge of one of the largest onion-growing operations in the country.

"People are dependent on us to make a living," Bruce says. Because of the popularity of locally grown produce, "farmers' markets and roadside stands are no longer a hobby. It's a business for them." Bruce understands that even for home gardeners, each order means someone will be on their hands and knees in their gardens planting an average of 10 bundles, with 50 to 70 plants per bundle.

Bruce says the most important consideration for growing good onions is selecting the right variety for your area of the country. If you plant short-day varieties in the northern states, the onions won't have enough time to make much top growth. If you plant long-day varieties in the southern states, the plants will keep making tops and won't ever form a bulb.

If you want to grow blue ribbon onions, you'll need to do a little math to make sure you get the timing right. "A perfect onion has 13 rings," Bruce says, and each ring corresponds to a leaf on the plant. "Plants arrive with 4 leaves, so they need to grow 9 [more] leaves. An onion shoots a new leaf

once every two weeks," he explains. So for great onions "you need 18 weeks of growing, which is 126 days or 4 months. June 21 is the vernal equinox, the longest day, so every onion will have to have started bulbing by then or not at all."

To figure your planting date, count back 126 days from that June date, which makes it difficult for onion growers in areas with short seasons. Bruce says it's hard to grow big onions because gardeners have to have their transplants in the ground by February 21. Most settle for equally perfect but smaller-sized onions.

Bruce says that although you need to speed up growing tops, overwatering isn't the answer. Selecting the right variety, having good loose soil, and fertilizing provide the best chance for success. Once plants have developed a good root system, they need a steady diet of nitrogen to make foliage and keep growing.

Anything that harms the leaves is a problem because the leaves affect the size and health of the bulb. So it's important to protect foliage from spores of harmful fungi. If onion diseases are a problem in your area, that might mean using an organic or synthetic fungicide to keep onion tops disease-free. "If you're east of the Mississippi, there's high humidity, and spores can be created within 10 hours of leaf wet," Bruce explains. Even if the weather then dries, he says, spores can survive on the ground. When it rains, the spores splash up and can reattach to the leaves.

As much as you may want to grow colossal onions to exhibit at the fair, in some parts of the country you simply can't grow extra-large onions. That's why Dixondale Farms also sells boxes of jumbo-sized sweet Texas onions for grilling instead of growing.

Short-day varieties do best in the warmer, southern part of the country (south of 35° latitude) where there are 10 to 12 hours of daylight in summer. Almost all short-day varieties are sweet onions. If you plant short-day varieties in the north, bulbs will start to form while plants are still small and so will never reach their full size.

Intermediate-day varieties, also known as day-neutral, need a long growing season but not extra-long days. They grow well in gardens located across the middle of the country. They'll form bulbs with 12 to 14 hours of daylight.

Long-day varieties do best in northern states (north of 35° latitude). They need 14 to 16 hours of daylight to start the bulbing process. If you live in the Deep South and plant long-day varieties, the onions won't have enough light to form bulbs.

GROWING GREAT ONIONS

Let's not mince words. If you want to grow blue-ribbon beauties, you'll to need to show your onion plants a lot of love. You'll want to grow healthy foliage, encourage bulb growth, and protect onions from pests and diseases. In addition to soil that's well amended with compost and other organic matter, onions need a consistent supply of fertilizer while they're growing. Some growers say onions may need as much as twice the amount of fertilizer as other garden-grown vegetables.

FEED FREQUENTLY

Remember "Feed Me, Seymour!" from the movie *Little Shop of Horrors*? That should be your refrain when it comes to onions. Before planting, prepare the bed with a fertilizer that's high in phosphorous to help encourage root growth and early bulb formation. Phosphorus

To push the limits of size, try planting a single onion in a container with very rich soil and a tomato cage to support the foliage.

also helps maintain the slim necks that are needed to win contests. (Potassium prevents thick necks, too.) A balanced fertilizer contains nitrogen, phosphorous, and potassium to keep plants healthy and growing.

In addition to selecting the right varieties and planting them at the right time, growing first-rate onions requires full sun, rich well-drained soil, plenty of water, adequate fertilizer, and room to grow. Onions can also be planted in raised beds if you want to plant earlier, because soil in raised beds tends to warm faster.

THE 1860 MINNESOTA STATE FAIR, at Fort Snelling, was a rousing success. Reports from the fair described exhibits featuring gigantic onions that were 17 inches in circumference, as well as "radishes 28 inches, squashes 5 feet and 5 inches, Irish potatoes a foot in length and four inches in diameter, and cabbage heads a single one of which could not be crowded into a flour barrel."

Onions will grow as big as their space allows. Plant onion seeds about ¼ inch deep; onion sets about 1 inch deep; and onion transplants 1 inch deep or deep enough to keep plants upright. Space plants so their roots can spread out (4 to 6 inches apart).

Once bulbs start forming, side-dress the bed with additional nutrients. Use a fertilizer with plenty of micronutrients or good-quality compost; apply in a shallow channel near the onion rows, and cover with soil. Take care to keep fertilizer away from the foliage and bulbs.

Keep soil evenly moist with a soaker hose. Don't let plants dry out or bulbs may split. If leaves start to turn yellow, plants may be getting too much water.

Use mulch to keep the onion bed weed-free; avoid cultivating or yanking up weeds that can disturb the onion's delicate root system. When onions start pushing the topsoil away, stop fertilizing. Some of the bulb will start to show above the soil, but resist the urge to re-cover it. As soon as onion tops begin to topple over, stop watering and get ready to harvest.

TOPS WILL TOPPLE

Dig onions when most of the green tops have fallen, but before the foliage dries completely. Carefully lift onions from the soil to prevent bruising or damaging the bulbs, and let them dry in the sun to cure. Protect bulbs against sunburn by letting the leaves of one row cover the bulbs in another. During wet or rainy weather, cure onions under cover or in a way that allows air to circulate above, below, and around bulbs.

Onions are cured when the tops, roots, and the top few layers of skin look dry. Make sure the

Tops falling over are a sign that onions are ready to be harvested.

CHECKLIST FOR
BLUE RIBBON DRY ONIONS

IF YOU'RE SHOWING IN any of the dry onion classes, harvest your onions several weeks in advance of the contest to allow the tops to dry completely. For the fair, choose mature onions (those that meet the size requirements) with intact, unblemished dry skin and small, well-dried necks. Remove loose, jagged, or dirty outer scales (the fleshy leaf bases) down to the first dry, fully colored scale.

PICK
- ☐ Large, firm, heavy onions
- ☐ True-to-type and uniform in size, color, and shape
- ☐ Smooth, clear scales
- ☐ Necks thin and well dried

PASS
- ☐ Immature or green bulbs
- ☐ Sprouting, split, or double bulbs
- ☐ Thick, soft necks
- ☐ Misshapen, diseased, or damaged bulbs

PRESENT
- ☐ Cut tops cleanly ½ to 1 inch above shoulder
- ☐ Leave on outer skin
- ☐ Don't wash; gently rub to clean while dry
- ☐ Trim roots to base of bulb

CoPRA

Onions must be thoroughly dried after harvest.

neck has lost all its moisture with the traditional farmer's test: rub the neck between your thumb and forefinger. Any hint of moisture will cause the neck to slide back and forth.

Wait until onions are thoroughly cured before cleaning and then gently brush off soil. Store on a flat surface, spread apart, in a cool dry place.

GROWING BUNCHING or GREEN ONIONS

Any onion can be harvested and used as a green onion if it's pulled while the bulb is immature. However for competition, your best bet is to plant *Allium fistulosum*, the species that's meant to grow bunching onions, also called scallions. Varieties like 'Evergreen Bunching' or 'Beltsville Bunching' grow the slender white onion stalks and hollow green leaves that judges will be looking for.

You can plant bunching onions as sets or as tiny onion seeds. For seeds, you can start indoors or plant them outside. Check the amount of time to maturity and start long-season varieties indoors well in advance of the last frost date (eight weeks or more).

Day length isn't a problem for green onions, because no bulbs will form. Plant onion seeds ¼ to ½ inch deep; and sets about 1 inch deep and 2 to 3 inches apart. Succession planting works well for bunching onions and ensures a continuous crop.

Give them plenty of sun. Water as needed with soaker hoses to help maintain consistent soil moisture. Mulch is a good idea, too. It's important to keep the soil evenly moist, not soggy, and to never let the soil completely dry — otherwise the onions can dry, too. Long white stems are especially attractive and can be helped along by slightly hilling soil around plants when their tops have grown to about 4 inches tall.

If you amended the garden bed with compost and well-aged manure, you'll need to add only a balanced fertilizer while green onions are growing.

Carefully dig green onions when the tops reach 6 to 8 inches tall and the necks meet the minimum diameter. Check the show book for the required number of onions needed in the bunch, the length of the trimmed stems, and where they should be tied (at the top, bottom, or both ends).

PREVENTING ONION PROBLEMS

An onion is a vegetable that can make you cry, especially when something goes wrong in the onion patch. But it's easy to avoid tears when growing onions, and here's how.

When choosing onion cultivars, look for those bred to resist downy mildew, pink root rot, thrips, and whatever onion enemies are common in your area. Good cultural practices will also go a long way toward preventing problems. Rotate where you grow your onion crops, plant onions in well-drained soil or raised beds, avoid crowding plants, maintain a weed-free garden, and keep plants watered. Pull up and toss any bulbs that stop growing or start to show disease problems.

Remember that anything that hurts the plant's leaves is going to affect the bulb. Work to keep leaves healthy and upright. Watch for these problems that can affect leaves and bulbs:

Onion flies lay eggs that grow into maggots, which tunnel into bulbs and stems. Prevent problems with onion maggots by rotating onion plantings every three or four years to keep from planting in the same spot. Rotating onion crops helps prevent recurring pest and disease problems. If you've seen these in past years, use row cover to exclude flies or apply beneficial nematodes to the soil to kill the maggots.

Onion thrips are small insects that suck the life out of leaves, and with a bad infestation, the plant can die. Thrips are almost too small to see, so look for symptoms: leaves that turn grey and then curl. Prevent by planting cultivars that are

CHECKLIST FOR BLUE RIBBON GREEN ONIONS

SHOW YOUR GREEN ONIONS in bunches with full tops and clipped roots. Select straight onions that are ⅜ to ¾ inch in diameter. Each base should be clean and white, with a straight, light green shank (with little to no swelling) and dark green flutes (leaves). Remove older outer leaves and thoroughly wash tops and roots; trim to the specified length.

PICK
- [ ] No bulbs or only slight bulbs
- [ ] Healthy, dark green leaves
- [ ] Long, straight, slender light green shanks

PASS
- [ ] Bulbs too skinny or enlarged
- [ ] Leaves dry or poor color
- [ ] Curved, bent, or discolored shanks
- [ ] Diseased or damaged onions

PRESENT
- [ ] Strip off loose or yellow leaves
- [ ] Remove any loose skin
- [ ] Cut tops and trim roots to specifications
- [ ] Rinse to clean

resistant to onion thrips. If you see symptoms, use neem or insecticidal soaps for control.

Alternaria blight is a fungal disease that causes the tips of foliage to turn brown and die. Look for resistant varieties and plant in well-drained soils or raised beds to keep it at bay.

Pink root is a soilborne fungal disease that causes stunted and discolored bulbs. The name comes from the color the roots turn as they rot. Where this disease is common, avoid planting onion sets, as these can carry the fungus, or plant resistant varieties.

Purple blotch, an airborne fungus, shows up as purplish discolorations on leaves and stunted bulbs. It spreads during wet weather. Space plants to allow good air circulation and avoid wetting foliage to keep plants healthy. If your plants become infected despite your best efforts, control with an appropriate fungicide.

Onion smut shows up on the leaves in the early stages of seedling growth. This fungal disease first appears as dark streaks that break open and release black powdery spores. Prevent this disease with a three- or four-year crop-rotation plan. Pull up and trash any diseased plants.

Onion mildew (downy mildew) usually shows up in midsummer, first as yellow spots on the upper part of leaves that eventually show as fuzzy mold. Mildew can impair bulb development. Prevent by planting in well-drained soil, keeping foliage dry, thinning/spacing to allow good air circulation, and planting mildew-resistant varieties. Fungicides may help.

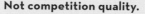

Not competition quality. Prizewinning onions obviously shouldn't be rotted! In order to present well, they should be trimmed to the length set out in your fair's show book. The papery outer layer of skin should be left intact.

GROW THE WORLD'S BIGGEST ONION RINGS

JUMBO ONION CONTESTS are part of the vegetable fun at state fairs, but the giant onion championships in the United Kingdom are serious business. Most competitors grow their giant onions under cover, using artificial light and heat. That's why the size of the winners has more than doubled over the last 25 years.

The top show for giant onions is the annual National Onion Championships held during the North of England Horticultural Society's autumn flower show. Peter Glazebrook is well known as a perennial winner, but his 18.1-pound world record onion was topped in 2014. That's when Tony Glover made it into *Guinness World Records* with his 18.11-pounder.

Peter Glazebrook and his award-winning onion

If you'd like to try growing giant onions, you need to get a few things right. Follow these tips:

Right seeds: Select a variety like 'Kelsae Sweet Giant', which typically grows 15-pound onions. This long-day cultivar was developed in Scotland in the 1950s. Plant four times the number of plants needed for the contest to ensure you'll have plenty of potential winners.

Right spot: Plant in a spot that gets as much sunlight as possible. In northern latitudes you can try growing onions in large containers in a greenhouse with supplemental lighting.

Right soil: Prepare a bed of rich soil that's deeply dug.

Right time: Plant seeds according to the time-table for your region; plant over several weeks.

Right space: Give each plant at least 2 feet of space so bulbs can really spread out. Construct a cage or supporting structure to keep leaves upright and protect them from wind, which can damage tender leaves.

Right care: Feed plants every two weeks after transplanting with high-nitrogen liquid fertilizer. Switch to a high-potassium fertilizer midsummer to help bulbs gain weight. Watch for insect and disease problems, and take action quickly to keep bulbs healthy. Count leaves to judge the size of your winner. The more leaves, the bigger the bulb, so aim for 20 or more.

Right harvest time: Because every ounce counts, giant onions should be harvested right before the contest to keep them as weighty as possible.

CHAPTER 10

PEPPERS

WOULD YOU LIKE A PECK OF PERFECT PEPPERS TO ENTER in the fair? Start by selecting the cultivars that will grow best in your climate. Peppers can be picky if they don't get just the right combination of hot days and enough time to ripen. Because the pepper classes are some of the most popular categories at vegetable competitions, look for new, unfamiliar, or unusual entries with the right amount of heat you like to eat.

LD WORLD DIETS in the 1490s must've been blander than a bowl of cold overcooked cabbage. Why else would chile peppers have spread like wildfire as soon they were discovered? Experts say it took less than 100 years for chile seeds to travel from the Americas to Europe, Africa, Asia, and back again. Compared to the amount of time it took other fruits and vegetables to expand their reach, chiles were an overnight sensation.

Chile peppers originated in Central and South America, where they still grow wild. Hungry birds, immune to pepper heat, helped spread seeds through Mexico. Then people helped move them farther north. When Columbus first tasted the dried and powdered spice he called it "pepper," thinking it was similar to black pepper. He was as wrong about peppers as he was about geography, but it didn't matter. People were already in love with the seasoning's flavor and heat, much as we are now.

> **GARDENERS CAN STILL** get their hands on seeds for the tiny pea-shaped chile called chiltepin, one of the original peppers still found growing wild in Mexico today.

Peppers are a member of the nightshade family (Solanaceae), just like tomatoes, eggplants, and potatoes. They're a perennial plant in tropical regions, but gardeners in other climates grow them as annuals. Most of the peppers grown are *Capsicum annuum*, but there are at least 20 other species of *Capsicum*, including tabasco (*C. frutescens*), habaneros and Scotch bonnets (*C. chinense*), and aji (*C. baccatum*).

PICK YOUR PEPPERS

While smaller fairs may only have classes for hot and sweet peppers, larger fairs (like the one in Iowa) have more. They might have an entire division dedicated to hot peppers, a contest for containers of pepper plants loaded with fruit, *and* a vegetable collection contest that includes all the peppers, tomatoes, onions, and herbs needed to make salsa.

SELECTING SWEET PEPPERS

Hundreds of cultivars of sweet peppers are on the market now, and new ones are introduced every year. Breeders continue to develop sweet peppers to meet gardeners' requests for earlier maturation, better disease resistance, bigger yields, and more flavor — even some that offer a tinge of heat. Contests typically have categories for several kinds based on shape: large, blocky bell types; thin, curved bull's horns; long, tapered 'Cubanelle' types; sweet banana peppers; and other sweets such as mini-bells, pimentos, and sweet cherry peppers.

Not all peppers will grow well in every part of the country. The best sweet peppers for competition are hybrids that are widely adapted and can consistently produce a good number of market-perfect peppers that are uniform in size and shape. Read seed and plant descriptions carefully for the clues that will offer you the best chance for success. If you garden in a cooler climate, look for short-season or early-maturing varieties. In a longer, hotter season, you may need peppers that are more disease resistant or that provide better foliage cover to prevent sunscald (pale spots on fruits from too much sun).

Depending on the cultivar, plants may produce as few as five peppers on each plant. Be sure to plant enough of each kind to ensure there will be enough ripe fruits to take to the contest.

Ask for recommendations from experienced pepper growers in your area, and see what wins the top prizes at the local fair. Check the All-America Selections winners list, and be on the lookout for new introductions that receive high marks in regional garden trials. Some old favorites with the classic blocky bell shape include 'California Wonder', 'Valencia', 'Golden Bell', and 'Mexibell'.

'PEPPERONCINI'

'TWEETY'

'THAI HOT'

'ORANGE BLAZE'

'CUTE STUFF'

'BORIS'

'ANCHO'

'BIG BOMB'

'SUPER CHILI'

POTENTIAL PRIZEWINNING PEPPERS

WHEN I STARTED GROWING PEPPERS in containers on my patio, it was because I didn't have any other garden space. Even now that I have plenty of planting places, I still enjoy growing peppers in pots. I like the convenience of having them right out the back door. Plus they're easy to plant and a cinch to maintain, and they can be moved around the patio if they need more sun, shade, or space. Some of my container-grown chiles have garnered blue ribbons, too. Here are my top pepper picks:

HOT CHILE PEPPERS
- 'Cayenne'
- 'Cayennetta'
- 'Fresno'
- 'Hungarian Paprika'
- 'Kung Pao'
- 'Mariachi'
- 'Mucho Nacho'
- 'NuMex Heritage 6-4'
- 'NuMex Joe E. Parker'
- 'Royal Black'
- 'Suribachi'
- 'Tabasco'

SWEET PEPPERS
- 'Gemini'
- 'King Arthur'
- 'Lipstick'
- 'Miniature Red Bell' (aka 'Red Mini-Bell')
- 'Mohawk'

Color is an especially important characteristic of sweet peppers. The majority start out green and with time will ripen to red, yellow, orange, purple, or brown. The key word is *time*. Once peppers have reached their full size, it can take as long as a month or more for them to turn the desired color. Some gardeners say they have better luck growing yellow or gold bell peppers, but you'll have to experiment to find what will grow best in your garden.

Here are some ideas that can help sweet peppers color up faster:

- Plant varieties with the shortest number of days to maturity.
- Look for "early-ripening" or "extra-early" varieties.
- Choose mini-bell or non-bell varieties.
- Try a yellow, ivory, or lavender cultivar.
- Make the most of warm, sheltered microclimates.
- Plant in raised beds that slope toward the sun.
- Clip peppers once they show some color, and let them ripen fully in a paper bag with an apple or tomato.

SELECTING HOT PEPPERS

If you have a burning desire to win a ribbon for your chile peppers, get in line. Peppers are one of the most competitive categories at vegetable contests. Need proof? There were 198 plates of hot peppers entered in the vegetable competition at the Iowa State Fair in 2013.

If you've never grown chile peppers, then it's time to bring on the heat. The most difficult part of growing them is choosing from the

THERE ARE SOME known sweet pepper heavyweights in the garden, like 'Big Bertha', 'Goliath', and 'Sweet Big Daddy'. But an ordinary bell pepper grown in Israel and nicknamed "Godzilla" set a green pepper record in 2013. It weighed in at more than 1 pound!

An array of hot peppers at the fair

fairs also have recipe contests for homemade salsas, barbecue sauces, condiments, and spicy mixes. Extreme hot pepper enthusiasts like to refer to themselves as "chileheads."

Read through your fair's show book to understand the different competitive classes for peppers. Some split classes by heat levels (fiery, hot, sweet, and warm). Others group the hot pepper entries by the shape of the pod or type of pepper (Thai, 'Cayenne', New Mexico or Anaheim, habanero, hot cherry, Hungarian wax or banana, jalapeño, poblano, serrano, and 'Mariachi' or 'Santa Fe Grande').

Chiles are a diverse group, and choosing potential prize-winners can be daunting. Start by considering the classes of peppers at the contest you want to enter and the length of your growing season. Then search seed and plant catalogs for interesting peppers that are known to do well in your region, have maturity dates that match your growing season and contest dates, and have the kind of heat you'd like to eat. Read chile descriptions for hints to their likelihood for success in your garden: strong plants; continuous set; disease/virus resistance; adaptable; uniform fruits; excellent yields; consistent high quality; large fruit; lengthy harvest; extremely prolific; early maturing; and so forth. Estimate the number of chiles you might get from each plant (5 to 25), and add a few more of each to ensure there'll be plenty of healthy pods to show.

thousands of kinds that include nearly every size, shape, color, and level of heat.

Chile pepper competitions have also grown beyond the boundaries of vegetable contests. There are jalapeño-eating contests, chili cook-offs, and the intense rivalry to see who can grow the world's hottest chile pepper. Many

THE PHARMACY OF HEAT

WHEN YOU TAKE A BITE of a habanero and it bites back, that's capsaicin at work. The pain receptors in your mouth are being fueled by this flavorless, tasteless alkaloid compound, which is manufactured in the pepper's ribs. While trying to create capsaicin-based medicines for the Parke-Davis pharmaceutical company in 1912, Wilbur Scoville, an American pharmacologist, developed a test to gauge the heat level of different peppers.

I applaud those courageous testers who lent their tongues to advance science. The test required tasting solutions of capsaicin extract and sugar water to rate the varying degrees of heat in different kinds of chiles. The Scoville Organoleptic Test, and the resulting ratio of sugar water to capsaicin, became the standard way to measure the heat of chile peppers. Testing showed pure capsaicin registered between 15 million and 16 million heat units on the Scoville scale; bell peppers start at 0. The hottest peppers typically come in the smallest packages, but you can't judge a pepper's heat by its size.

PEPPERS AND THEIR SCOVILLE HEAT UNITS

PEPPER	SCOVILLE HEAT UNITS	USES
Bell pepper	0–1,000	Adds flavor but not much heat to many kinds of cooking.
Poblano	1,000–2000	Becomes sweeter as it ripens to a reddish brown; when dried it's called an ancho pepper. When roasted it makes a rich mole sauce.
Anaheim (aka New Mexico)	0–7000	Gives a mild chile taste for Mexican cuisine; used in chile rellenos and green chile sauces.
Jalapeño	0–50,000	Adds heat and spicy flavor when used raw, roasted, or stuffed.
Chile de árbol	30,000–50,000	Powerful chiles that can be used fresh, dried, or ground into powder.
Habanero	80,000–150,000	Dangerously hot orange peppers — a little goes a long way for flavoring sauces.

BRING ON THE HEAT!

ONE YEAR I INADVERTENTLY
discovered what it takes to turn a relatively warm chile into something unseasonably hot — just like the weather that summer. Peppers that are a little stressed will grow hotter fruits than pampered plants. You may get fewer and smaller peppers, but they'll have more concentrated heat. Here are a few tips to bring on the heat for a hot-pepper tasting contest:

- Check the average number of 95°F days for your region. Because peppers are tropical plants, the more days they sweat it out in high temperatures, the hotter they'll be.
- Pick a hot spot. Find ways to increase the temperature in already-warm microclimates. For example, plant chiles in black containers and place them in full sun on a concrete patio.
- Start with a known quantity. Pick a pepper with a relatively high heat value. Plant a superhot chile — at your own risk!
- Plan ahead for a long season. Some chiles can take a month or more to sprout and will then need at least 100 days to mature.
- Plant in a soil that drains quickly, ideally a sandy loam. No need to add compost; hold back on fertilizers high in nitrogen.
- Be stingy and water only when plants start to wilt.
- Pick later. Keep peppers on the plant as long as possible. The riper they get, the hotter they'll be.

GROWING GREAT PEPPERS

Even the most experienced pepper grower can be stymied by the weather. First, peppers are sensitive to temperature extremes. They grow best when temperatures are between 60 and 85°F, and they'll stop growing when temperatures are hotter or colder. Gardeners in hot climates may want to try shade cloth to overcome temperature extremes and to help prevent sunscald; a light-colored mulch will also help keep soil temperatures cool. Second, peppers become more colorful and flavorful the longer they remain on the plant, so you'll need to plan additional time to let them ripen to the clear, deep colors that win contests.

Start with healthy transplants that will grow into large sturdy plants. If you're starting from seeds, plan for 10 to 12 weeks to get to them to the transplanting stage. Bottom heat can help speed germination. An alternative is to buy transplants. When shopping for pepper plants, look for short stocky specimens with dark green leaves and no flowers or fruit. You can now buy pepper plants that have been grafted onto tough tomato rootstocks. Though more expensive, the resulting pepper plants are more resistant to soilborne diseases.

TRANSPLANTING AND MAINTAINING

Because peppers are tropical plants, they need warmth to germinate and to grow, so you can't transplant until a week or two after the last frost date. Wait for the garden soil to warm and for nighttime temperatures to be a steady 50 to 55°F. Cold temperatures can set back plant growth, cause blossom drop, or result in misshapen fruit. Reduce transplant shock by gradually acclimating plants to the outdoors for a week or so before planting. You can get started sooner by warming the soil with water-filled plant protectors or other season extenders. Need a warmer microclimate for your peppers? Plant near a south-facing wall or fence to give peppers extra heat overnight.

Choose a sunny part of the garden where you haven't grown peppers, tomatoes, eggplants, or potatoes for at least two years. Set plants in well-amended and well-drained soil. Give each plant about 18 to 24 inches of garden space. Or plant in containers; one plant per 2- to 5-gallon container (with drainage holes) works for average-sized plants. And provide some form of support. Just like tomatoes, pepper plants need to be staked to keep them upright.

Get plants growing quickly with a well-balanced fertilizer. Peppers need nitrogen to encourage a big, leafy plant that will grow a good crop of fruit; phosphorus for establishing roots and flowering; and potassium to help form strong fruits and increase disease resistance. Feed as needed through the season with an extra boost in mid-July. Keep soil moist, but not soggy. Allow the soil to dry slightly between watering; peppers like things just a bit drier than other blue ribbon vegetables.

Pepper plants grow very well in warm soil; covering the bed in plastic will increase the soil temperature and help the plants become more productive.

'Orange Blaze'

CHECKLIST FOR BLUE RIBBON SWEET PEPPERS

SWEET PEPPER SPECIMENS should be full size, firm, and uniform in size, shape, and number of lobes (two, three, or four). If exhibiting colorful peppers, make sure they have shiny skin and uniform rich color with no green showing. Cut fruit from plants leaving long stems, and then trim according to contest guidelines.

PICK
- ☐ Large, firm peppers heavy for their size
- ☐ Uniform in number of lobes, color, size, and shape
- ☐ Unblemished skin

PASS
- ☐ Immature (small) peppers
- ☐ Lightweight, limp, wilted, or damaged
- ☐ Soft or bruised spots, scrapes, or insect damage
- ☐ Inconsistent coloring

PRESENT
- ☐ Clean with a soft cloth
- ☐ Trim stem cleanly to specified length

HARVESTING

If you've planted enough pepper plants, you should have a good selection of pods to pick. And by picking, I mean using pruners to carefully snip pods from the plant. Look for firm peppers that are symmetrical and uniform in size, shape, and color. If you have enough peppers, check one for freshness by breaking in two with your hands. It should have a satisfying snap. Leave stems attached, and make sure the length of stem meets contest rules. Clean, but don't polish, peppers.

While the season is still early, harvest some peppers before they ripen to help encourage plants to keep producing. Pepper plants will keep producing as long as you keep picking the produce. You'll need to leave some on the plant though if you want to take ripe and deeply colored peppers to the fair.

Sometimes judges cut through the middle of a pepper to peek inside, or slice peppers lengthwise to see if fruits are fully developed and at the peak of maturity. Some brave judges may even do a taste test. These in-depth examinations are the best way for judges to differentiate between several high-quality pepper entries and take a closer look at a specimen from each entry.

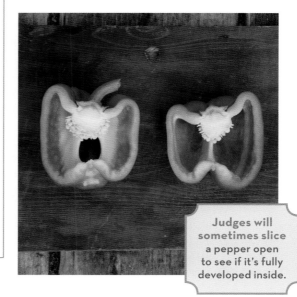

Judges will sometimes slice a pepper open to see if it's fully developed inside.

NEW CULTIVARS CAN FUEL COMPETITIVE FEVER

IF YOU'VE EVER GROWN a New Mexican–type chile pepper in your garden, you're connected to cultivars developed at New Mexico State University (NMSU) over the last 100 years. These flavorful chiles are not just an essential ingredient in southwestern cuisine; they're also a boon to chile growers and home gardeners alike. The university's chile pepper breeding program has led to the introduction of dozens of new cultivars with improved flavor, more consistent heat, better disease resistance, and bigger yields.

NuMex Peppers

Many of the chiles developed at the university, located in Las Cruces, use the NuMex descriptor to set them apart from others on the market. 'NuMex Heritage Big Jim' and 'NuMex Heritage 6-4' have more flavor and aroma than the older varieties used to create them. The new varieties also fuel the growing interest in heirloom varieties, explains Dr. Paul Bosland, professor of horticulture and a leader in the university's chile breeding and genetics research program. As cofounder and director of the university's Chile Pepper Institute, Dr. Bosland has spent more than 20 years working at the only research-based resource for chile peppers in the world.

"One of the greatest accomplishments at the Chile Pepper Institute is educating people about the heat profiles, flavor, and the thousands of chiles out there," he says.

To help with that, Dr. Bosland devised a way to describe a chile pepper's profile. It's surprising to learn that a pepper's intensity, measured in Scoville heat units, is actually last on his list. The five heat profile elements include how the heat develops (immediate or delayed), its duration (a short time or lingering), where the heat is located in the mouth (lips, mid-palate, throat), the kind of feeling it gives on the tongue (pinpricks or broad strokes), and *then* its intensity.

You can purchase the institute's Chile Flavor Wheel to help sort through 14 of the most popular types of chiles, from aji to 'Tabasco'. Even the 'Bhut Jolokia' is a featured pepper. Spin the wheel to learn about each pod type, species, cultivars, heat profile, flavor, and uses. The wheel could be an especially valuable tool if you want to match chile peppers to your individual taste — or to the tastes of judges at a contest.

Competing with Potted Peppers

If you're interested in entering competitions with a potted pepper plant sporting fruit, you might try some of the special line of dwarf ornamentals developed at NMSU. These colorful peppers sit upright on plants and ripen to colors that celebrate holidays. 'NuMex Easter', an All-America Selections bedding plant winner in 2014, features peppers that mature in hues from lavender to light yellow to orange.

"ONE OF THE GREATEST ACCOMPLISHMENTS at the Chile Pepper Institute is educating people about the heat profiles, flavor, and the thousands of chiles out there." — Dr. Bosland

Styrofoam produce crates are a great way to safely transport vegetables to the fair.

For the best chance at a blue ribbon, you want pepper walls that are firm and the right thickness for the variety. Stems and calyxes should be fresh and green. Veins, placenta, and seeds should be well formed and not under-ripe or overly ripe.

PREVENTING PEPPER PROBLEMS

PHYSIOLOGICAL ISSUES

Good cultural practices help prevent most pepper problems. Rotate where you grow your pepper crops; don't plant them where peppers or tomatoes (or eggplant or potatoes) grew in the past two seasons, especially if any of those had problems with diseases.

Blossom-end rot is caused by calcium deficiencies and moisture irregularities. Water as needed to keep soil evenly moist. A soil test may help; blossom-end rot is less of a problem when soil pH is 6.5 or greater.

Sunscald can disfigure fruits on plants with sparse foliage. Look for robust varieties known to produce abundant foliage. Encourage a leafy canopy with a balanced fertilizer. In hot climates you may need to protect plants from intense sunlight with row cover or another kind of shade.

INSECT PESTS

It pays to keep an eye on the pepper plants for any potential problems. It's rare for anything to kill a plant, but you could lose some of your crop or end up with peppers that aren't prize-worthy. The same insects that attack tomatoes can also be attracted to peppers: aphids, cutworms, flea beetles, and slugs.

Aphids are tiny pests that cluster on new growth and cause damage by sucking sap from plants. Watch for ants crawling on plants because they're attracted to honeydew that aphids leave behind. A blast of water from the hose every few days will spray aphids away.

CHECKLIST FOR BLUE RIBBON
HOT PEPPERS

SELECT FULL-SIZE, CRISP, AND SOLID FRUITS that are uniform in size and color. Carefully clip peppers from plants, leaving enough stem to trim to the required length. If fruits aren't identical in size, place them on the plate like a fan, with slightly smaller peppers on each end.

PICK
☐ Firm, shapely peppers that are true to type
☐ Uniform in length, color, and size
☐ Unblemished skin

PASS
☐ Lightweight or immature peppers
☐ Cracks, soft spots, or damage
☐ Missing or dried stems and calyxes

PRESENT
☐ Trim stems to specified length from shoulder (usually ¼ to 1 inch)
☐ Clean with a soft, dry cloth

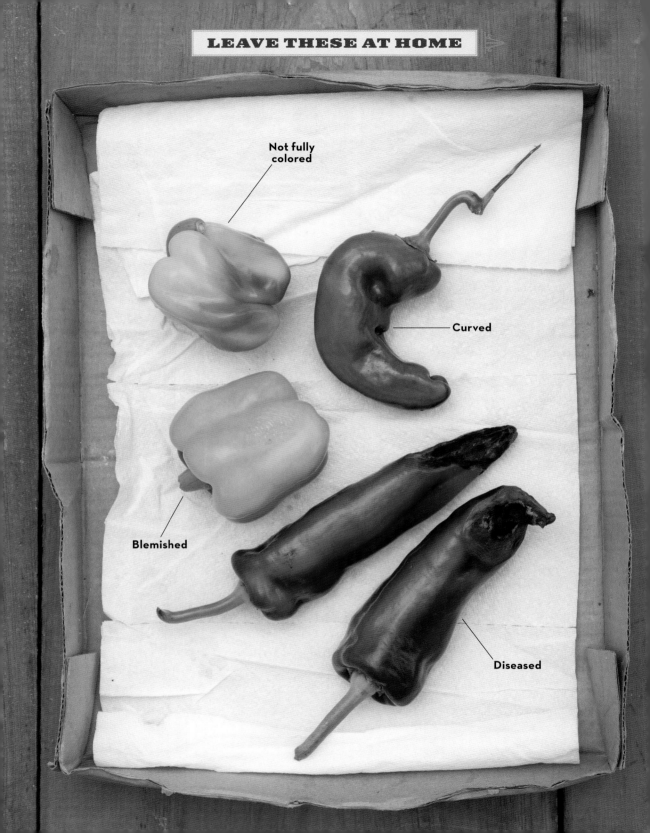

Not fully
colored

Curved

Blemished

Diseased

Cutworms like tender transplants and can take down a young pepper overnight. Protect pepper transplants by placing collars around the stems at planting time.

Flea beetles can make leaves look like they've been hit with buckshot, so stop them before they get started. Exclude flea beetles by covering plants with row cover cloth sealed at the edges, or cover individual plants. Remove when flowering begins to allow for pollination.

Slugs usually appear after periods of wet weather and will eat seedlings, leaves, and ripe fruit. Trap slugs by pouring beer into a shallow dish placed on the ground near plants, or sprinkle diatomaceous earth on the soil around plant stems.

DISEASES

Peppers are susceptible to a few diseases. Prevent problems by selecting cultivars that offer good disease resistance, especially when planting sweet peppers. Look for "resistant to TMV," "good resistance to phytophtora," or "good disease protection" in seed and plant descriptions. Here are the most common pepper diseases:

Anthracnose is a fungal disease that can start as dark spots on leaves and stems and then spread to cause sunken spots on pepper pods. The fungal spores can be blown into gardens or spread by insects. To avoid, plant resistant cultivars, rotate pepper crops, and destroy any infected plant parts.

Tobacco mosaic virus (TMV) infects a number of fruiting vegetables, including peppers. Look for leaves that are mottled, puckered, or twisted. The virus causes stunted plants that perform poorly. In addition to planting TMV-resistant pepper cultivars, keep the garden weeded to prevent insects from picking up

the virus and spreading it through the garden. Destroy infected plants.

Bacterial spot can cause leaf drop and spotting that can ruin pepper pods. This bacterial disease first appears as green bumps on the undersides of leaves and eventually causes small water-soaked brown spots on pods. Reduce the risk of bacterial spot by planting healthy transplants and avoiding working in the garden while leaves are wet. Pull up and destroy diseased plants.

Phytophthora is a fungus-like pathogen that can affect plant roots, leaves, and fruits. Affected plants will wilt and eventually die. Look for dark lesions on pepper plant stems near the soil line. Destroy diseased plants to prevent spreading the blight to other plants. Prevent phytophthora by rotating crops in the pepper family, planting peppers in well-drained soil, and avoiding excessive watering.

Fruits that come in contact with the ground are much more susceptible to pests and diseases.

PUMPKINS

IS THERE ANOTHER VEGETABLE WITH AS MUCH MYSTIQUE

as the pumpkin? There aren't any tales about a magic cucumber carriage, and we don't wait for The Great Onion to appear each Halloween. Pumpkins are often the first vegetables kids learn to grow because the seeds are big and the results even bigger. Pumpkin experts happily share their growing tips, whether you want to grow a perfect jack-o'-lantern or an unimaginable orange giant.

FOR HORTICULTURAL COM-PETITIONS, the main difference between a pumpkin and a squash is the stem. Pumpkins have hard, square woody stems; squash have round and tender stems. Vegetable contest rules may specify whether pumpkin entries need to be orange and have a woody (ribbed) stem, or if entries can be a green squash-type pumpkin. For some contests, any *Cucurbita* may be considered a pumpkin.

Pumpkin contest classes typically include a sugar, pie, or culinary type; a miniature or ornamental; a field or jack-o'-lantern type;

and a jumbo. The best pumpkins in any class are those that are mature, deeply colored, symmetrical, and blemish-free.

Some contests also include a decorative class for carved, painted, or scarred fruit. Scarred pumpkins are intentionally disfigured; they have healed-over embellishments that were cut into the pumpkin while it was still growing in the field or garden.

If you want to make an impression at the fair, exhibit the Cinderella pumpkin. 'Rouge Vif d'Etampes' is a beautiful French heirloom that served as the model for the pumpkin carriage in the familiar fairy tale.

GIANTS AMONG US

Giant pumpkins are usually entered in a separate contest, and it's not a beauty contest either. One of the most vivid (and politically incorrect) images I've read describing a giant pumpkin comes from Michael Leapman's book *The Biggest Beetroot in the World*. In Leapman's words, a giant pumpkin is more telegenic than a long carrot because of its "bright amber skin and shape faintly reminiscent of a fat lady's bottom on a saucy seaside postcard."

Giant pumpkins are judged by weight, and prize money is significantly more than in other pumpkin contests. Some giant pumpkin weigh-offs have a minimum weight for specimens or require an attached five-sided stem to prove it's not a squash. Many giant pumpkin weigh-offs are events sanctioned by the Great Pumpkin Commonwealth (GPC), an international organization that developed standards and regulations for weigh-offs around the world.

Other qualities besides weight can determine jumbo pumpkin winners. Contests for the largest pumpkin are judged by measuring around the fruit from stem to blossom end and also around the midsection. The sum of these two measurements gives the total number of inches. In case of a tie, the pumpkin that weighs the most is declared the winner.

WILD GOURDS

PUMPKIN ANCESTORS didn't hold quite the appeal their modern-day relatives do. The wild *Cucurbita pepo* gourds that originated in South and Central America were small with bitter flesh. The only edible parts were the oil-rich seeds, and the gourds were more useful as containers than food.

It took many years for humans to develop pumpkins into the colorful round fruits we celebrate today. The early-cultivated pumpkins were probably lumpy on the outside and stringy and bland on the inside. Surely the Pilgrims had to learn to love or at least tolerate the texture and taste of pumpkins if they wanted to survive those first trying winters.

Of the cultivated pumpkin-type *Cucurbita*, gardeners are most familiar with varieties of *C. pepo*. These are ones we grow into jack-o'-lanterns. Another common species is *C. moschata*; it includes pumpkins and winter squash. *Cucurbita maxima* includes pumpkins that can reach mammoth proportions.

Pumpkin stems are square and woody; squash stems are round and tender.

A GIANT HISTORY

For more than 150 years, growers have amazed their friends and neighbors by hauling unbelievably large pumpkins to garden shows and exhibitions. One of the first giant pumpkins on record was a 245-pound 'Mammoth' squash that made a big impact at a horticulture event in Devonshire, England, in 1857. Around the same time, writer and naturalist Henry David Thoreau won a prize at the Middlesex Fair in Massachusetts for his 123-pound pumpkin, a variety from France known as the 'Jaune Gros de Paris'.

Farmers and gardeners kept trying to grow bigger pumpkins. In 1893 William Warnock, a Canadian gardener, took the agricultural world by surprise with the 365-pound pumpkin he exhibited at the Chicago World's Fair. He set another record in 1900 at the Paris World's Fair with a 400-pounder. A few years later at the St. Louis World's Fair, he beat his own record again with a hefty 403-pound pumpkin.

It took more than 70 years for another grower to unseat that heavyweight. In 1980, an amateur seed breeder in Nova Scotia cracked the code and changed the world of giant pumpkin growing forever. Inspired by the big pumpkins his father entered in local agricultural fairs, Howard Dill worked to develop a giant pumpkin, and he succeeded with a 459-pound monster. Ever since then, growers planting 'Dill's Atlantic Giant' seeds or Atlantic crosses have set giant pumpkin records that now top more than 2,000 pounds.

CUCURBITA MAXIMA: Even its name sounds big. And it was a big day in 1996 when the first 1,000-pound giant pumpkin tipped the scale. As soon as that record was in the books, growers set their sights on a 1,500-pounder. Then in 2012 Ron Wallace, a Rhode Island grower, broke the 2,000-pound barrier!

GROWING GREAT PUMPKINS

Most pumpkins take from 90 to more than 100 days to mature, so you'll need to get started

early if you want to enter a contest. Find the average last frost date for your region, and start seeds indoors about two weeks before that date or plan on direct-sowing seeds in the garden. Wait until the soil has warmed for planting, or speed warming by covering soil with black plastic. Some short-season gardeners transplant pumpkins into a hoop house, a tunnel, or another protected growing environment. Be sure to acclimate seedlings before transplanting into the garden.

As with other members of the squash or gourd family (Cucurbitaceae), pumpkins grow well in rich well-drained soil, so incorporate lots of compost before planting time. When transplanting into the garden, be especially careful not to damage the plant's roots. Pumpkins can take up a lot of garden real estate, so give vines plenty of room to grow and to keep vines from crossing over each other. Plant seeds 1 inch deep in small hills with three to five seeds in each hill. Space hills so miniature or ornamental pumpkin plants will be about 2 or 3 feet apart; larger pumpkins, about 5 or 6 feet apart. Once plants

start to grow, thin each hill to the sturdiest-looking two or three plants.

Reduce as many environmental stressors as possible. Keep soil evenly moist with drip or soaker irrigation to avoid getting leaves and vines wet. Use mulch to keep beds weed-free and conserve soil moisture. Never let the soil dry completely, or vines can wilt, which causes pumpkin problems such as small or soft fruits.

Because pumpkins are heavy feeders, they'll need nutrients through the season. Use a balanced fertilizer at planting time. Every three weeks, feed with your favorite plant food, whether that's compost, well-rotted manure, or a liquid fertilizer.

A lopsided pumpkin or one with a light-colored grow spot on its belly won't win any prizes. To prevent flat spots, gently place the maturing fruit on a wooden board or plank to keep it off the ground, and regularly rotate it while it's growing. Whenever lifting or moving pumpkins, take great care not to break or damage the stem. For small pumpkins with

Marty Schnicker covers his giant pumpkin to protect it from the sun.

perfect skin, grow them on trellises and use old nylons or other soft material to cradle and support the fruit.

SPECIAL CARE FOR ROOTS AND SHOOTS

To grow a picture-perfect pumpkin requires more than just planting seeds and letting vines grow wild. A beautiful specimen grows on a plant with healthy roots and shoots, and it pays to know the basics of how a pumpkin grows.

You may be surprised to learn the plant's root system is just as extensive (and essential) as the aboveground vines and foliage. Even vines of small pumpkins can reach 16 feet long, with roots filling the top 12 inches of soil. Taproots of mature pumpkins can travel 6 feet deep and spread as wide as the vines to create a complex root system. Keep an image of this root system in mind to help you understand that roots need to be tended with careful cultivation, fertilizing, and deep watering.

It's important to nurture and protect all the parts of a pumpkin plant. Protect shallow roots belowground by using mulch to control weeds. Prevent root damage by pulling weeds carefully by hand. Aboveground, try to avoid compacting soil, and don't walk on or over vines.

Pumpkin leaves and stems need attention, too. Keep vines healthy with regular feedings of a balanced fertilizer. Bury the leaf nodes that form along runners to help them form new roots.

Nearly all pumpkin growers employ a few tricks to improve their efforts. Some remove all the female flowers for the first few weeks to foster sturdier vines that set more pumpkins. Other growers prefer fewer, but larger, fruits and leave only a few fruits on the vine, preventing others from forming by pinching off new flowers as they

GIANT PUMP-KINS CAN PUT ON 30 TO 40 POUNDS A DAY. But if they grow too quickly, they can explode and scatter seeds 6 feet away.

Placing a plastic plate under the young pumpkin will help protect it from soil-dwelling insect pests and soil-borne diseases.

form. To grow bigger fruit, borrow a page from the giant pumpkin growers and prune your vines. Here's how:

- Allow the main vines to grow until pumpkins start to form.
- Prune the secondary vines or runners that grow from the main vine at the base of each leaf stem. Make your cut 10 to 12 feet along the secondary vine, from the point where it joins the main vine.
- Cover the cut end of each secondary vine with soil. Covering in this way helps reduce water loss and keeps disease from entering the plant through the cut.
- Cut off the tertiary vines that grow from the secondary vines. Removing these vines promotes fruit growth instead of plant growth. Cut each tertiary vine where it intersects with the secondary runner. Remove any new tertiary vine growth as soon as it starts to develop.
- Cut the main vines 10 to 15 feet beyond the last pumpkin on the vine; leave the largest pumpkin on each main vine and remove smaller pumpkins as they start to form. Be sure to bury the cut end of the main vine with a layer of soil.

CHECKLIST FOR BLUE RIBBON PUMPKINS

IF YOU'VE EVER SEARCHED for the perfect pumpkin to carve into a Halloween jack-o'-lantern, you know an ideal fruit when you see it, even if it's a miniature version. The pumpkin should be well formed, thick fleshed, and well cured. Most field pumpkins have a hard, dark orange skin with a cleanly cut stem where it was attached to the vine.

PICK
- ☐ Pumpkins with a hard rind and heavy for their size
- ☐ True to type in size, shape, and color
- ☐ Unblemished skin

PASS
- ☐ Missing stem
- ☐ Lightweight for its size
- ☐ Scratches, scars, or damage

PRESENT
- ☐ Trim stem to required length
- ☐ Remove soil with a soft, moist cloth

GET YOUR PUMPKIN GROWING

Every grower takes a different approach to cultivating giant pumpkins, but here's what you'll need to get started:

A big pumpkin patch. If you want to grow a 400-pounder, you'll need at least a 10-foot by 10-foot growing area, or a 20-by-20-foot patch for anything bigger.

Superb soil and fertilizer. It all starts with soil that's tested and amended and tested again. To improve the soil, start by adding lots of compost. Or you can plant cover crops the previous season and turn them under, to grow your own organic matter in place. Apply fertilizers in well-timed applications through the season.

Special seeds. Choose seeds that have the potential to grow a giant, like 'Atlantic Giant' or 'Goliath Giant'.

Plenty of time. Plan on 140 days or more from starting seeds indoors to harvesting for the weigh-off.

Attention to detail. Protect your pumpkins from frost, wind, heat, hail, sun scorch, and other stressors. Many growers construct elaborate structures, with automatic misting, irrigating, and fertilizing systems to create an ideal growing environment.

Staying power. Plan on spending long days watering, pollinating, fertilizing, pruning, repositioning, watching for diseases, and fending off pests of all sizes.

Reckoning. Keep an eye on the size of your specimens. Measure the largest circumference (stem to blossom end), the widest distance from one side to the other, and the length of the pumpkin from stem to blossom end. The higher the number of total inches, the weightier the gourd.

'Jack Be Little'

POTENTIAL PRIZEWINNING PUMPKINS

ALL-AMERICA SELECTIONS has a long history of selecting pumpkins as vegetable winners, starting in 1952 with 'Allneck Cushaw'. This variety looks more like a winter squash with its rounded bulb bottom and tapered neck. An article in the *Pittsburgh Press* announced all the AAS winners in January of that year, including this silver medal winner. As the paper reported, "The accompanying picture of this vegetable shows very graphically the derivation of its name." To let the gourd times roll, try these AAS pumpkin winners; they have performed especially well in trial gardens across the country.

- 'Autumn Gold'
- 'Baby Bear'
- 'Cinderella's Carriage'
- 'Hijinks'
- 'Jack Be Little'
- 'Orange Smoothie'
- 'Sorcerer'
- 'Spirit'

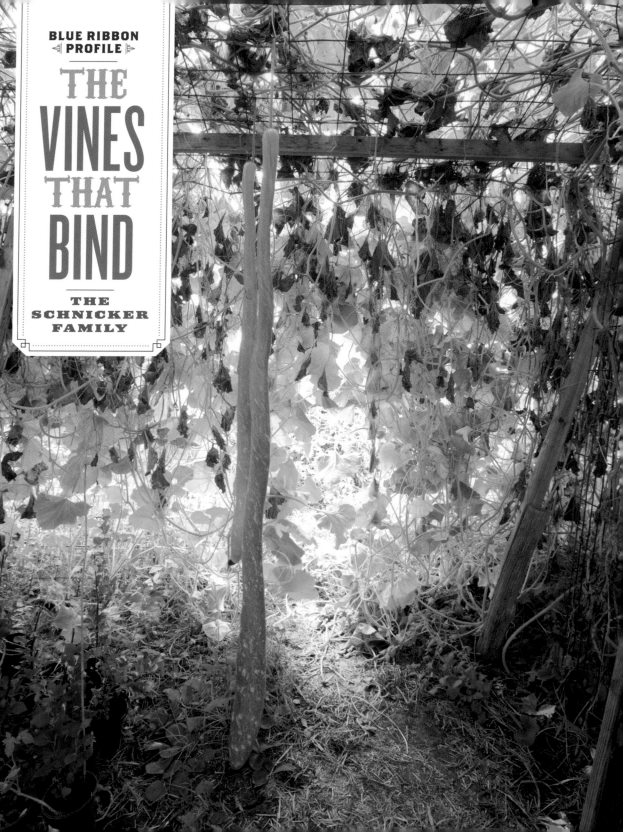

THE VINES THAT BIND

THE SCHNICKER FAMILY

GROWING JUMBO FRUITS AND VEGETABLES IS A FAMILY AFFAIR

at the Schnickers' home in Mount Pleasant, Iowa. Marty, his wife, Mary, and their six children work together to grow as many giant vegetables as they can. "I've always had a fascination with pumpkins and trying to grow them as big as I can," says Marty. He planted his first 'Dill's Atlantic Giant' seeds in 2004 and grew a 908-pound pumpkin.

Since then, he's grown all kinds of jumbo fruits and vegetables to enter in the Iowa State Fair. His many prizewinners include a pumpkin weighing 1,099 pounds, a 30-pound kohlrabi, a 180-pound watermelon, a 90-pound cabbage, and a 3.5-pound tomato. His prizewinning 5.2-pound onion was so big that one ring filled up a skillet!

The Schnickers have a large garden on their 5 acres, and all of the kids — toddlers to teens — pitch in. Chores include hand-pollinating, weeding, and helping at the family's booth at the farmers' market for a cut of the profits. They stretch their creativity by growing gourds and turning them into money-making craft projects, too. All of the work in the garden adds up, Marty says, and it helps the kids "understand money, how to grow vegetables, and what it takes to grow blue ribbon vegetables."

There's a big incentive, too. Instead of getting an allowance, the kids accumulate points for working in the garden. The points can be redeemed for fun activities, like spending time at a friend's house or going somewhere with Dad. Marty says the point system keeps things even: no work, no points. "People ask how we do it and I tell them, 'One kid gets a row and another gets another row.' Now they all want their own garden."

One downside of getting so much help in the garden is that Marty rarely gets to see any peas. Though they plant 20 rows of peas, the kids either eat them right off the vines or fill their pockets full.

"Growing the jumbo vegetables is a novelty and we enjoy doing it," Marty explains. In addition to growing giant fruits and vegetables to

enter in the fair, he raises several 100- to 300-pound pumpkins for the kids each year.

For those who want to try growing a giant pumpkin, Marty has some advice. Always select the best seeds possible; those usually come from another giant pumpkin grower. Give plants plenty of room to grow, and protect them from wind and harsh conditions. "We cover the pumpkins with a tarp or white sheet to keep the sun off and to keep them soft as they grow so fast," he relates. "Keep checking daily because so many things can go wrong, like rodents, deer, and even a goat can have a meal on a young pumpkin," he says. "If it was easy, everyone would do it."

Marty is well versed in the challenges of trying to grow a giant pumpkin. Giant pumpkins should be in the ground by April 1, but some years snow is still on the ground in May. He's seen pumpkins that weigh over 1,200 pounds split trying to put on 50 pounds in one day. He's also experienced the heartbreak of having pumpkins split in the truck on the way to the fair.

It takes patience to grow prizewinning giants. "If you bomb out in July, you have to wait another year," Marty says. But "when you see the ribbons go on, it's worth it. The kids get more excited than I do."

It's a major undertaking to move a 1,000-pound pumpkin from the field to the fair without harming the pumpkin or the helpers who handle it.

Transportation and a "heavy gang." It takes plenty of planning and friend power to carefully remove a giant from the garden. Line up your moving crew well in advance so they're in place on the day of the contest.

Record keeping and research. Keep detailed records of your efforts, including the type of seeds you planted, planting dates, fertilizing schedule, and weather data. Also note problems such as insect and diseases plus what treatments you used. And of course, record measurements of your best specimens!

Growing giants is a year-round activity. You can't get pumpkins to grow over 1,000 pounds without a lot of physical and mental effort. The big growers spend much of their spare time reading, studying, discussing, and dreaming of ways to improve their results.

HARVESTING

As the time for the fair approaches, check pumpkins for ripeness. Before harvesting, use your fingers to "thump" the fruit and listen for a hollow sound. Another test is to gently push a fingernail into the skin; too soft means it's not ripe.

Use a sharp knife or pruners to cut pumpkins from their vines, and be sure to leave several inches of stem attached — but don't break the stem by using it to lift or carry the pumpkin. Give pumpkins time to cure ahead of the contest by leaving them outside in a protected space for several days, or about a week indoors. If the weather is dry and warm (80 to 85°F), leave pumpkins outside to cure in the sun for up to two weeks. Protect from wet weather, cold nights, and frost by moving them into a garage or shed. Or cure indoors in a spot where there's good ventilation and air can circulate around the fruit.

PREVENTING PUMPKIN PROBLEMS

Plan ahead to protect your plants. Rotate where you grow all your *Cucurbita* crops, and plant disease-resistant cultivars. Make sure plants have good soil drainage and plenty of space between for air to circulate. Know how to spot the most common pumpkin pests and diseases in your region, and be ready to tackle problems quickly. Keep leaves healthy by checking the undersides for insect eggs and treating as needed.

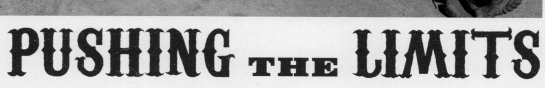

PUSHING THE LIMITS

SO EXACTLY HOW BIG CAN A PUMPKIN GET? "They'll continue to get bigger because we're isolating genetics and refining techniques," says Gary Grande. He's president and CEO of the Rocky Mountain Giant Vegetable Growers (RMGVG), an organization in Littleton, Colorado. "There's got to be a limit somewhere, but we haven't found it yet," he claims.

Gary got serious about growing giant pumpkins in 2006, after an especially cruel hailstorm ruined the promise of a potential prizewinner. Intent on learning ways to avoid such problems in the future, he started ColoradoPumpkins.com and organized the RMGVG group to encourage interest in growing giant pumpkins. The club started with a handful of members, and like the pumpkins themselves, it has grown exponentially since.

Even though giant-pumpkin growers are competitors by nature, most are willing to share information, resources, advice, and even seeds. Growers spend much of their off-season carefully studying genetic lines to select seeds from past winners. One of the beneficiaries of Gary's generosity is Grace Lusty, a youngster in New Zealand, who found RMGVG through the group's Facebook page. Gary gave her a club membership and her first batch of giant pumpkin seeds. Seeds sent from other club members spurred on Grace's own pumpkin challenge efforts as she in turn handed out seed packets to more than 60 other kids. Now the Great Pumpkin Commonwealth is holding sanctioned weigh-off events Down Under.

Gary admits luck is one of the keys to growing big pumpkins. "Because you're working with Mother Nature, we like to say, 'the harder one works, the luckier one gets.' You have to be slow and steady, too," he advises.

"I've always been fascinated with growing pumpkins, the way they grow, the challenge to do better each year," Gary says. He also likes to share the information with others, admitting that "even if they end up growing bigger [pumpkins] than you, there's an accomplishment in that."

You can dodge some pests by growing shorter-season pumpkins and delay planting until the first wave of insect pests passes through. Use row covers to protect young plants. Other tried-and-true control methods include sticky traps and handpicking larger insects (drop them into a jar of soapy water). Despite your best efforts, you may find yourself with some questions. Here are some answers:

- **Pumpkin flowers not setting fruit?** When vines first start to flower, there are more male than female blossoms. It's normal for these to fall off the vine. If you notice the female flowers are falling, it's because they weren't pollinated. Pollinate by hand: transfer pollen from a male flower to a few of the female flowers. (See Sex and the Single Cucumber, page 107.)
- **White powdery stuff on pumpkin leaves?** It's likely to be powdery mildew, a fungal disease that can harm leaves and cause pumpkins to ripen improperly. Pick off diseased leaves. Prevent powdery mildew by keeping soil moisture high and watering early in the morning with drip irrigation or a soaker hose to avoid wetting leaves.
- **Small yellow-and-black insects on plants?** Cucumber beetles (see page 186) can suck the life right out of your pumpkin plants. They attack seedlings and vines, and in late summer they can attack mature pumpkins, scarring the fruit. Check the large leaves regularly and take action as soon as you see tiny red eggs. Handpick and destroy adults and eggs. Spray plants with a garlic–red pepper spray or insecticidal soap.
- **Brownish insects on plants?** Squash bugs attack stems, leaves, and fruit causing the plant to wilt and die. Handpick bugs and their eggs and destroy. Place boards on the ground near plants and the pests will gather under the boards for collecting in the morning. Exclude bugs by covering transplants

with row cover. Be sure the edges are sealed so bugs can't find their way in; remove cover when flowers begin to form to allow for pollination.
- **Leaves on vines turned bright yellow and then suddenly wilted?** Sounds like yellow vine decline, a bacterial disease spread by squash bugs. Control the bugs to prevent the disease (see above).
- **White spots on pumpkins' leaves and stems?** This could be a blight-like fungal disease that can show up in wet, rainy weather. It can cause leaves to drop and small bumps to form on pumpkins. The fungus can live in the soil, so rotate where you plant pumpkins (and other crops in the squash family) to prevent the problem.
- **Sawdust-like shavings on the ground?** A squash vine borer has likely burrowed into the pumpkin stem. This pest can cause the vines to suddenly wilt and die. Handpick and destroy any of the small, white wormlike larvae, or eggs that look like little reddish-brown dots.

Prevent attacks by covering planted areas and transplants with row cover to keep moths from laying eggs. Reduce chances of attack by growing healthy vines and encouraging as many secondary runners as possible. Cover the lower 6 inches of stem with cloth or other material to exclude the borer's eggs. Prevent problems in the future by planting resistant cultivars.

CHAPTER 12

SQUASH

THERE'S NO ONE WAY TO GROW SPECTACULAR SQUASHES, because every squash seed contains prizewinning potential. It pays to match each squash's maturity date to your growing season and to give each plant a steady supply of high-quality fertilizer. Challenge yourself to plant and grow some unusual summer squashes and some new-to-you heirloom winter squashes, too. If you enter a few in every contest category, you just might come home with a heaping helping of honors.

QUASH IS JUST ONE member of a big clan that also includes pumpkins, cucumbers, melons, and gourds. Some say the gourd family (Cucurbitaceae) is the most important plant family because of all it provides: countless flavorful fruits, protein-rich seeds, edible roots, tough fibers, everyday utensils, and beautiful autumn decorations.

Squashes have been around for quite a while. Archeologists in Mexico have found seeds and gourd remains that are believed to be seven thousand years old. Wild squash species were domesticated in South America (*Cucurbita maxima*) and Mexico (*C. ficifolia*, *C. moschata*, and *C. mixta*). The familiar *C. pepo* may have been domesticated twice, once in northeastern Mexico and once by Native Americans further north.

In the 1490s, transoceanic voyagers collected specimens and transported them back to their homelands, from which seeds were carried to other countries. By the turn of the sixteenth century, Europeans were enjoying squashes and pumpkins, too. Some of the hundreds of squashes we enjoy today are the result of chance crosses; others come to us after years of shrewd breeding for more uniform shapes and improved colors, tastes, textures, and disease resistance.

Some of the most stunning entries in a vegetable competition are the ones gardeners grow for the squash contests. Whether an out-of-the-ordinary smooth-skinned summer squash or a winter squash you could wear as a hat, there are dozens of ways to wow the crowd in the squash category.

SUMMER SQUASH BASICS

Most summer squashes belong to the *Cucurbita pepo* species. These typically grow on short-vining bushes and can reach competition size in about 40 days. There are several groups of summer squash: crookneck, scallop, straightneck, and zucchini.

'Elite'

POTENTIAL PRIZEWINNING SUMMER SQUASH

PLANT BREEDERS ARE TAKING some of the fun out of growing summer squash, what with cultivars that have more upright habits, fewer (or no) spines, and fruit that stays at a prime-eating size longer. Selecting the squashes you want to grow is matter of taste and available garden space. Here are some tried-and-true varieties:

ZUCCHINI
- 'Aristocrat'
- 'Black Beauty'
- 'Chefini'

YELLOW STRAIGHTNECK
- 'Early Prolific Straightneck'
- 'Goldbar'
- 'Gold Rush'

YELLOW CROOKNECK
- 'Early Summer Crookneck'
- 'Yellow Crookneck'

SCALLOP
- 'Peter Pan'
- 'Starship'
- 'Sunburst'

'SUNBURST'

'ENTERPRISE F₁'

'ONE BALL'

'AUTUMN DELIGHT'

'YUGOSLAVIAN FINGERS'

VEGETABLE SPAGHETTI

'RED KABOCHA'

'PINK BANANA'

'HASTA LA PASTA'

'BLUE HUBBARD'

Contests may have classes for all or just a few of the summer squash groups. Most often there will be classes for yellow crookneck and straightneck; white scallop or patty pan; and yellow and green zucchini. The "other" category for squashes allows you to show unusual kinds, like round squashes that range in size from cue ball to softball.

Summer squashes are always shown at their immature stage, and contest rules may specify a certain length and diameter. For example, rules may specify that yellow straightnecks should be 5 to 6 inches long; zucchini, 6 to 9 inches long; and scallop types, 3 to 4 inches in diameter. If your squashes get away from you, don't fret. Many contests encourage exhibitors to enter their overmature or extra-large specimens in the jumbo vegetable contest.

Rules typically require each entry to be exhibited with its stem. Judges will be looking for blemish-free skin, firm light-colored flesh, and immature seeds. Before the contest, slice into a sample to make sure seeds are still small and soft.

WINTER SQUASH BASICS

Winter squashes can include species of *Cucurbita pepo*, *C. maxima*, and *C. moschata*. These squashes grow on long vines and develop a hard rind that allows for storing in winter. Some of the common competition classes of winter squashes include acorn, acorn-like, banana, buttercup, butternut, 'Delicata', Hubbard, and spaghetti. Some squashes look a lot like their pumpkin relatives, but pumpkins have hard stems and squashes have softer, round stems.

Winter squashes are shown at their mature stage. They can take 100 days to be ready to exhibit, depending on the variety. No matter their size, all winter squash entries need to have a hard, firm outer rind, deep color typical of the variety, and an attached length of stem. The flesh should be solid, and seeds should be hard and mature.

'Carnival'

POTENTIAL PRIZEWINNING WINTER SQUASH

THE WINTER SQUASH CATEGORY makes for some of the most interesting exhibits at any vegetable competition. Here are some of the many colorful characters for growing and showing:

ACORN
- 'Cream of the Crop'
- 'Fordhook'
- 'Honey Bear'
- 'Table King'

BANANA
- 'Guatemalan Blue Banana'
- 'Jumbo Pink Banana'
- 'Sibley'

BUTTERNUT
- 'Butterbush'
- 'Early Butternut'
- 'Waltham'

BUTTERCUP
- 'Autumn Cup'
- 'Burgess Buttercup'
- 'Discus Bush Buttercup'

HUBBARD OR HUBBARD-TYPE
- 'Blue Hubbard'
- 'Sugar Hubbard'
- 'Sweet Meat'

SPAGHETTI
- 'Hasta la Pasta'
- 'Small Wonder'
- 'Tivoli'

SAVING THE FAMILY JEWELS

TODAY YOU CAN GROW some of the same squashes that American farmers exhibited during the 1800s, because people saved their seeds and passed them along. Thanks to their diligent seed-saving efforts, you can still grow a 'Red Warty Thing' to take to the county fair.

'Red Warty Thing' is an old Hubbard-type winter squash first introduced as 'Victor' in the late 1890s. Recently this variety has been rediscovered, renamed, and revered. "We grew one in 2013 that was the biggest plant I've ever seen," says Bryan Stuart, field manager at Seed Savers Exchange (SSE) in Decorah, Iowa. "The fruit was probably 4 or 5 feet around, but it [the plant] had a wingspan of about 30 feet in each direction. It took over the whole garden, but it's a beautiful fruit."

The upper Midwest is a challenging place to grow squashes for seed production because of the humid climate and short growing season. Bryan and his crew have to wait for the weather to warm sufficiently in spring before planting. Some of their best practices for growing the selected squashes include planting under row cover until plants start to flower. Then they remove the row cover and begin hand-pollinating to ensure a pure line of seeds.

The staff at the 890-acre farm uses only organic methods to control insect pests like cucumber beetles. Insecticides containing pyrethrins, derived from chrysanthemums, and kaolin clay work well.

In September the crew may prune squash vines, to signal plants to stop vegetative growth and start maturing the seeds inside the fruit. The squashes are left in the field as long as possible.

"We do everything the old-fashioned way, by hand," Bryan says. "We split the fruit in half and dig out the seed by hand." Seeds are washed, rinsed, and dried on old window screens before being transferred to a climate-controlled cold room. After testing, they're moved into the freezer for long-term storage.

SSE also sends seeds to other seed banks for long-term backup storage. Some go to the USDA's National Center for Genetic Resources Preservation seed bank in Fort Collins, Colorado; others, to the Svalbard Global Seed Vault that's buried deep inside a mountain on an island that belongs to Norway.

The continuing work of passionate preservationists means generations of gardeners will get to plant the same heirloom squashes that someone's great-grandmother, grandpa, or uncle grew and treasured many years ago. "An important part of preservation is the more that are doing it, the better it works," Bryan says. "We're maintaining a lot of family history, good breeding work, and the work people put into developing these varieties. If we weren't preserving them," he adds, "they'd be lost forever."

GROWING GREAT SQUASH

The summer I started my first vegetable garden, I planted six zucchini plants. I really like fresh zucchini, and I wanted to make sure I'd have enough to enjoy in all my favorite forms: fresh, fried, baked, and stuffed. That was the same year I discovered that one healthy plant can grow enough zucchini to feed the world.

To say zucchini is prolific is an understatement. These fruits practically grow themselves. At the height of the season, they can be ready to pick within a week of flowering. It can be challenging to keep up with them, but they need to be harvested early and often to keep plants productive (and to avoid tripping over club-sized lunkers lurking beneath the leaves).

Squash is easy to grow, if you simply give plants what they need. Because they originated in a hot climate, summer squashes grow best during hot weather. Wait until the soil and weather have warmed before direct sowing or transplanting.

Squash also needs lots of room, so allow plenty of garden space for plants or vines to spread out. Shorter vines can be trained to grow up stakes, and long vines can be grown on strong trellises. Vertical gardening helps keep plants healthy and protects delicate skin in the process. An added benefit of growing squash vertically is that the large leaves are especially ornamental.

Patio and balcony gardeners can grow summer squash for showing, too. New cultivars bred specifically for container growing feature full-size squash on smaller plants. Some even grow on shorter vines. You just may need to plant a few more to make sure you have enough specimens to take to the fair.

Another important consideration is that squash plants are especially hungry and can eat anything. Massachusetts seedsman James J. H. Gregory made that point clear in his

1867 book *Squashes: How to Grow Them*. "The squash vine is a rank feeder," he wrote. "Night soil, barn manure, wood ashes, guano, mussel mud, hen manure, superphosphate of lime, pig manure, fish guano, fish waste — either of these alone, or in compost, is greedily devoured by this miscellaneous feeder. The great error in the cultivating of squash is to starve it." (*Note:* "night soil" is a euphemism for humanure;

please don't use this old-fashioned fertilizer to feed your squashes or anything else in your garden. Mussel mud — the marine sediment collected from the bottom of inlets and stream beds at low tide — is safer, but today you have easier alternatives.)

Squash plants need male and female blossoms present at the same time for pollination. To increase the likelihood for pollination, plant several of the same kinds of squash. Also add herbs and flowers that attract bees to your garden, or be prepared to hand-pollinate. (For more on hand-pollination, see Sex and the Single Cucumber, page 107.) Another alternative is to plant parthenocarpic varieties of squash; these are self-pollinating and don't need the services of bees.

TIPS FOR PLANTING SUMMER SQUASH

Depending on the variety, most summer squashes are ready to harvest in 40 to 60 days. Some gardeners ensure a continuous harvest by planting a crop for an early harvest and planting another in midsummer for a second round of fresh plants and fruit that will be ready at fair time. Staggered planting times can also help avoid some pest problems.

Plant squash in a sunny location. Amend the soil with compost, well-rotted manure, or other source of organic matter to ensure soil is fertile and well drained. If you have clayey soil, plant on slightly raised hills to help water drain away from seedlings to keep them healthy.

Where the growing season is short, plant seeds indoors in individual peat pots that can be transplanted into the garden. Start seeds about three weeks ahead of the last average frost date, but wait to transplant until the soil has warmed and the danger of frost has passed. Harden off seedlings to prevent transplant shock.

Where the growing season is longer, you can direct sow outdoors. Plant four to six seeds as a group, 1 inch deep, either on the top of the garden soil, in slight wells, or on slightly mounded hills. Allow at least 3 to 6 feet between plants (3 feet for bush varieties, more for older and larger varieties).

Mulch with black plastic or organic materials to keep weeds to a minimum. If you must cultivate the soil, do so carefully to keep from harming shallow roots.

THIS FESTIVAL FEATURES FAST FRUIT

WONDERING WHAT TO DO with your 5-pound zucchini after the competition? At the annual Boulder Creek Hometown Festival in Boulder, Colorado, contestants in the Great Zucchini Race pay a fee to decorate a mammoth zuke and pit it against others for prizes and bragging rights. The young drivers take their time selecting what they hope will be the most aerodynamically perfect zucchini for their heat. Volunteers hammer wheels on squashes before kids paint cars in garish colors, decorate them with feathers, and sprinkle on glitter for good luck. The first zucchini race car that makes it down the steep incline and across the finish line without wiping out is declared the winner.

This supersize zucchini may be bordering on inedible, but it's on its way to being a contender for the jumbo competition.

After seeds sprout, thin to the strongest two or three plants, spaced evenly apart. Small garden tunnels (row cover over short hoops) can protect seedlings for several weeks until it's time for them to start growing in earnest. Remove row cover once flowers appear; you don't want to prevent pollination.

Water squash deeply about once a week, especially while plants are blossoming and fruit is developing. To prevent foliar damage, avoid getting leaves wet.

Because squashes are heavy feeders, they benefit from additional applications of compost or a balanced fertilizer. Dig in or side-dress plants with compost when they start to blossom and while fruit is setting.

HARVESTING SUMMER SQUASH

As soon as plants start to set fruit, check vines daily. Harvest summer squash while they're still immature and the skin is shiny. Wear long sleeves and gloves to protect your hands and arms from spiny stems, and carefully cut squash from plants with pruning shears or a sharp knife. Leave enough stem to trim before the contest.

Check contest rules that specify the length or diameter of fruit to exhibit and clip when your squash are at their peak. Harvest fruits when they're at the desired size, even if it's a few days before the contest, and then keep fruit refrigerated and dry. Use plastic wrap or a moisture-proof container to prevent storage decay. Don't wash specimens before the contest, but wipe gently with a damp cloth. Handle with care. The skin of summer squash is easily scratched.

GROW A GIANT MARROW

Vegetable marrows are a summer squash (*Cucurbita pepo*) with a long history at horticultural exhibitions in the United Kingdom. Gardeners there work all summer to grow

CHECKLIST FOR BLUE RIBBON SUMMER SQUASH

WHEN IT'S CLOSE TO contest time, check squash plants daily, harvest right-size fruits, and keep them refrigerated until showtime. Clip with long stems so you can trim them before the contest for a just-cut look. There may be additional guidelines depending on whether you're showing yellow crookneck, yellow straightneck, or scallop varieties.

PICK
- ☐ Immature squash with tender, glossy, undamaged skin
- ☐ Uniform in size, shape, and color
- ☐ True to type in size, shape, and color

PASS
- ☐ Oversized or overmature
- ☐ Damaged, scratched, or blemished skin
- ☐ Missing or broken stem
- ☐ Soft spots
- ☐ Shriveled, limp squash

PRESENT
- ☐ Trim stems to required length
- ☐ Clean gently with a soft cloth

them as big as they can. It's a shame these giants aren't more popular with gardeners in the States. Marrows are easy to grow and can reach humongous proportions in about 75 days. Marrows are zucchini-like except for two points: they grow on long vines instead of bushes, and the ones grown for size have deep ridges.

In his book *How to Grow Giant Vegetables*, Bernard Lavery says, "If you have never attempted to grow a giant marrow, I do urge you to have a go; you could end up with some real monsters that will amaze yourself as well as dumbfound your friends." Lavery is well known in the United Kingdom as a giant vegetable expert. He's considered the father of giant vegetable growing, setting 25 world records and 37 British records before retiring in 1996. One of the many vegetable records he set was for the 108-pound marrow he grew in 1990.

In the 1800s gardeners dug deep pits and planted marrow varieties like 'Long White',

'Moore's Vegetable Cream', and 'Pen-y-Byd' in manure-heated hotbeds. Lavery took the sport to another level and suggested growing marrows in a large glasshouse or polythene growing tunnel, or possibly in the open garden. His recommendations include placing boards or planks to use as walkways near the plants to keep from damaging their delicate root system and allowing only three good marrows to grow along the main stem of the plant. Lavery suggests weekly applications of a high-nitrogen liquid fertilizer to the main roots until harvest. He also advises caution when harvesting. The marrows may be easy to cut from their vines, "but they can weigh much more than you might imagine."

If you'd like to grow your own record-setting squash, start with giant marrow seeds that are meant to grow into huge specimens. Some other summer squashes can also grow to more than 40 pounds. Look for a banana type such as 'Jumbo Pink Banana', or just let one of your zucchinis grow wild.

> When a winter squash turns yellow on the bottom, where it rests on the soil, it's ready to be harvested.

SAVING
SQUASH SEEDS

IF YOU WANT TO SAVE SEEDS from a prize-winning squash, you need to start at the beginning of the season. Squashes, pumpkins, and gourds can cross-pollinate with other varieties of the same species: *Cucurbita pepo* with other *C. pepo* varieties, or *C. maxima* types with other *C. maxima*. Cross-pollination won't affect the fruit from the current season, but will show up if you save seeds and plant them the following season. To keep your squash seeds pure, you need to control pollination. It's easy: keep flowers covered until right before they open, pollinate by hand, and tape the female flower closed as the fruit starts to grow.

TIPS FOR PLANTING WINTER SQUASH

Winter squashes take about twice as long to grow and mature as summer squashes (80 to 100 days). Be sure to count back the number of days from the contest and find squashes that will mature in your timeframe.

Winter squashes also take more space in the garden. Vines need 5 to 10 feet between hills, so follow spacing instructions carefully. Plant four to five seeds per grouping, about 1 inch deep. Thin to the strongest two or three plants when they're well established. Cover with short tunnels until vines start to push up on the cover. Mulch or use shallow cultivation to keep the garden weed-free.

HARVESTING WINTER SQUASH

Winter squashes are ready to harvest when they've reached their mature size and both stem and leaves are drying. The deep-colored skin will start to lose its shine and turn dull,

These summer squash mutants haven't developed their color properly and won't show well at the fair.

PREVENTING SQUASH PROBLEMS

Your best bet for growing healthy squash is to stay one step ahead of the game. As with other vegetables, it makes sense to seek out resistant varieties. You now have several options for zucchinis that are resistant to powdery mildew, for example. Rotate where you grow all your *Cucurbita* crops (squash, pumpkins, gourds). Grow squash in well-drained soil; incorporate lots of compost or other organic matter before planting to improve soil drainage (and help maintain soil moisture). Mulch also helps to conserve soil moisture and it keeps down weeds.

Provide adequate plant spacing to allow air to circulate. Water as needed to maintain good soil moisture (especially after fruit set). Learn the most common squash pests and diseases in your region, and take action if you spot trouble. Check leaf undersides for insect eggs. If you can't handpick the pests, you may need to remove a severely infested plant to protect the others. Here are some issues that might crop up with your squash plants:

and the shell should be hard enough to resist piercing with a fingernail.

Carefully cut squash from the vine with pruning shears or a sharp knife, leaving a bit of vine attached to several inches of stem. Lift heavy squash from the bottom (not the stem) to prevent damage. Handle winter squash gently to prevent nicks, cuts, bruises, or other damage that will detract from the specimen.

Mature winter squashes like Hubbard, butternut, buttercup, and spaghetti need to be cured before you take them to the fair. Curing sounds difficult, but all it means is storing your winter squash at room temperature, with good air circulation, for about two weeks. Curing helps the squash dry and skin harden for long-term storage. Cure in a well-ventilated area, like a basement, shed, or garage, until it's time to head to the fair.

- **Problems with new squash blossoms, shoots, and buds?** Pickleworms are the larvae of a night-flying moth and are the likely culprit if something has tunneled into buds, stalks, vines, or fruit. Use row covers

Spotted cucumber beetle

CHECKLIST FOR BLUE RIBBON
WINTER SQUASH

BEFORE HARVESTING WINTER SQUASHES, check the show book for any specific requirements. For example, butternut squash may need to display a thick, straight neck in proportion to the bulb end; acorn squash may need to show a deep yellow grow spot where the fruit was sitting on the ground. All winter squashes should be colorful and have a hard, well-cured shell that resists piercing with a fingernail.

PICK
- ☐ Squashes heavy for their size, with a hard rind
- ☐ Well-developed color
- ☐ Uniform size, shape, and color
- ☐ True to type in size, shape, and color

PASS
- ☐ Immature fruit
- ☐ Missing or soft stem
- ☐ Damaged or blemished rind

PRESENT
- ☐ Trim stem to required length
- ☐ Clean with a soft cloth

to prevent moths from laying eggs, especially at night. Applications of Bt may help control larvae. Destroy infected vines.

• **Small yellow-and-black striped or spotted insects?** Cucumber beetles love to eat seedlings, blossoms, and fruit. They can strip plants practically overnight, and they spread diseases like bacterial wilt and mosaic virus. If you can, delay planting in early spring to avoid the first wave of adults. Use yellow sticky traps to capture the pests.

• **Gray to dark brown, hard-shelled insects on leaves?** Squash bugs can suck juices from squash leaves (especially on winter squash); they can also spread disease. Check the undersides of leaves for eggs that are brownish red and found in clusters of 15 or more. Handpick and destroy the eggs.

• **Small, white grubs chewing their way into stems?** Squash vine borers are the larvae of a clear-winged moth (which doesn't look anything like a moth). Adults don't feed on plants, but they lay eggs that grow into the small white larvae that attack squash stems, causing sudden wilting of part of a vine. Sometimes they attack the fruit as well. Keep an eye out for small reddish eggs that grow into the wormlike larvae. Protect with row cover, or plant squash cultivars that are resistant.

• **Irregularly shaped spots on leaves and fruit?** Angular leaf spot is a bacterial disease that spreads rapidly by rain, hail, and contaminated equipment. Rotate crops of the squash family, water at soil level to avoid wetting leaves, and avoid working with or touching wet plants.

• **New foliage that shows up mottled or malformed?** It's most likely cucumber mosaic virus. Treat aphids that spread the disease with a strong blast of water from the hose. Keep squash beds weed-free and immediately remove and destroy any infected plants.

• **Flowers fall without forming fruits?** As with other cucurbits (e.g., cucumbers and pumpkins), you may need to help with pollination if blossoms drop or fruit dries and withers on the vine. For instructions on hand-pollination, see Sex and the Single Cucumber, page 107.

• **Fruits rot at the end opposite the stem?** Blossom-end rot on fruit is typically caused by lack of adequate soil moisture. Water as needed to maintain adequate moisture.

• **Spots or mold on leaves?** Bacterial wilt, leaf blights, viruses, and powdery and downy mildew are diseases that can harm plant leaves and ruin a squash crop. Affected leaves can die, leaving fruits exposed to sunscald, which damages tender skin and prevents squashes from maturing properly. Plant resistant cultivars, use good cultural practices, and water at ground level.

Powdery mildew

SQUASHING
THE COMPETITION

AMY GOLDMAN
FOWLER

AMY GOLDMAN FOWLER, AWARD-WINNING AUTHOR of *The Compleat Squash: A Passionate Grower's Guide to Pumpkins, Squashes, and Gourds*, entered her first vegetable competition in 1990 at the urging of a neighbor, an Englishwoman. This neighbor, who had experience competing in the floral division at the Dutchess County Fair in Rhinebeck, New York, said, "Look at all you grow. Come with me and I'll show you the ropes." So, on a lark, she did. "No one was more surprised to get a ribbon," Amy admits. "When you win those ribbons, it's good, positive reinforcement."

The next year Amy doubled the number of prizes she won, including a first-place ribbon for a 'Blue Hubbard' squash and an award of merit for her 'Dill's Atlantic Giant' pumpkin.

"What I learned that year about squash," she says, "is what judges value. Here they value size and table quality. It's the bigger the better, and I had a pretty humongo one."

Because she has only 150 frost-free days, she starts squash and pumpkins inside, and she uses plastic mulch to speed up growth. To prevent insects and diseases from taking their toll on the plants, she "babies them with row covers to beat the first wave of insects." There's also "a lot of hand-crushing of some critters," she adds. "It's all a race against time."

In 1995, during the 150th year of the Dutchess County Fair, she received the Grand Championship award after winning 38 blue ribbons in the vegetable classes. That total included 15 ribbons for her squashes alone. "No other vegetable dominated the contest like squashes and pumpkins, so I knew I'd have to master them to win," she says. "I also had a 440-pound 'Atlantic Giant'," Amy says. "I actually cried when I had to cut it from the vine, but it won."

To protect their delicate skin, she grew her summer squashes into plastic bags. Before each contest she'd harvest, clean, plate, label, and refrigerate them and then match them up right before the fair. She turned her garage into a curing shed for the winter squashes.

All of the squashes she grew were heirloom, open-pollinated, or standard varieties. "They're classics," she explains. "I don't think any hybrid can do better, and in some classes there's no hybrid that can compete." She's a great fan of heirloom varieties, saying "people overgeneralize that heirlooms are more difficult to grow, and I don't think that's the case. I highly recommend them."

Amy encourages other gardeners to plant heirloom and open-pollinated squash varieties through her ongoing work with the nonprofit Seed Savers Exchange. She participates both as seed saver and special advisor to its board of directors.

After winning the Grand Champion award at the 1996 New York State Fair, she competed only sporadically and never went for the big prize again. "I achieved what I set out to do," she says. "It can be all-consuming, but I loved it, especially after the judging. The fair is in a part of the country where agriculture is valued, so there's excitement on the part of the competitors and the fairgoers alike. That's why fairs were started in the first place, to keep agriculture alive."

"WHAT I LEARNED THAT YEAR ABOUT SQUASH IS WHAT JUDGES VALUE. HERE THEY VALUE SIZE AND TABLE QUALITY. IT'S THE BIGGER THE BETTER, AND I HAD A PRETTY HUMONGO ONE."

—AMY GOLDMAN FOWLER

CHAPTER 13

TOMATOES

SOME GARDENERS HAVE A LOVE-HATE RELATIONSHIP WITH growing tomatoes. They love the taste of a freshly picked home-grown tomato, but hate the problems — from diseases to pests — that stand between them and the ripe fruits. An award-winning tomato crop just needs warm weather, regular fertilizing, and the right amount of water. In other words, cultivate good gardening practices, and you will be rewarded.

ILD TOMATOES STARTED out somewhere in South America, perhaps along the warm coastal areas of Ecuador and Peru or in the Andes Mountains. The pre-Mayan people of Central America began domesticating and cultivating the fruit before the arrival of the conquistadors, who discovered *xitomatl* and carried specimens home to Spain. Tomatoes then traveled to Italy, southern France, and beyond. By the 1500s, botanists included images of deeply ribbed tomatoes in beautifully illustrated books about medicinal plants and herbs. Because they were unsure how to categorize these plants of the nightshade family, they grouped tomatoes in with poisonous jimsonweed, henbane, and deadly nightshade.

Instead of growing tomatoes to eat, gardeners valued them as ornamentals. Eventually brave souls tasted tomatoes and lived to tell others about it. In the mid-1800s a Harvard-trained physician by the name of Diocletian ("Dio") Lewis lectured healthy people against consuming tomatoes as a food. Instead he advised folks to eat small quantities of cooked tomatoes for medicinal purposes only. After years of being misunderstood, the tomato finally realized its potential as an important food crop in the nineteenth century.

Tomatoes are now the most popular edible gardeners grow. They certainly deserve their Love Apple nickname, but not for their rumored qualities as an aphrodisiac. People are head-over-heels in love with the delectable taste of these garden-grown globes of goodness.

Tomatoes aren't any more difficult to grow than other edibles, it just seems that way because so many folks try to grow them. Over the years I've answered more questions about growing tomatoes than about any other fruit or vegetable. People ask, "Why do tomatoes drop their blossoms?" or "Why do my tomatoes taste watery?" and "Do squirrels eat tomatoes?"

Tomatoes are tender, warm-season plants. All they need is a sunny space; a long growing season; fertile, well-drained soil; and enough water and nutrients to grow, flower, and produce fruit. And yes, squirrels love tomatoes too.

TOMATO TALK

With several thousand tomato selections available, there's sure to be at least one must-grow for everyone out there. If you ask gardeners about their favorites, be prepared to spend some time talking tomatoes. You'll hear about pint-sized currant, grape, and cherry tomatoes; medium slicers; and beefsteaks that can grow as large as a softball. Some gardeners sing the praises of heirlooms while others extol the benefits of growing hybrids.

Varieties are available for short, medium, and long growing seasons. There are bush tomatoes perfect for growing on patios, and tomatoes that grow in hanging baskets. Tomatoes come in a rainbow of colors: red, orange, yellow, green, black, indigo, pink, white, and bicolored.

With so many tomato varieties on the market and more introduced every year, it can be difficult to decide which kind to plant. Read descriptions carefully, looking for irresistible varieties that sound like real winners. Choose tomatoes by matching varieties to the length of your growing season, the weather conditions typical for your area of the country, and the size and type of tomatoes you like to eat.

Before making your final choices, check the show book to make sure there are categories for your selections in the contests you want to enter. The fair may offer as many as a dozen tomato classes, which may include beefsteak, paste, cherry, grape, and pear-shaped tomatoes. There may be classes for colors other than red, too.

Some contests include a special division for heirlooms or open-pollinated and nonhybrid

'VIVA ITALIA'

'GERMAN HEIRLOOM'

'CELEBRITY'

'JULIET'

'LEMON BOY'

'YELLOW PEAR'

'SUGARY'

varieties. For the entry tag in such classes, you may need to know the variety or include some historical detail such as the family name of the originating seed contributor. Other specialty tomato contests include the tastiest tomatoes, vegetable trays that include tomatoes, and jumbo or giant tomato contests (judged only by weight).

LEARN THE LINGO

When shopping for tomatoes, descriptions will include information on the size of the plant and disease resistance, as well as information on the fruits. Tomatoes are classified by their growth habit: determinate or indeterminate.

Determinate varieties are sometimes called bush tomatoes. Determinate plants are naturally limited to a certain size, usually shorter and more compact. These tomato plants set one good harvest of fruit over a short period of time, and then they call it quits. Some gardeners grow determinate varieties of paste tomatoes so they'll have a large amount of tomatoes that ripen at the same time for canning, or enough to enter in several contests scheduled close together.

Indeterminate, or vining-type, tomatoes have no natural size restrictions, so plants grow taller and wider. Plants set fruit, vines continue to grow, and the plant keeps producing tomatoes through the season. If you're planning on competing, indeterminate varieties will produce tomatoes over a longer period of time, so you can enter multiple fairs and contests. You may have fewer tomatoes at any one time, though.

To head off common tomato problems, look for cultivars described as disease resistant (or at least tolerant). Many modern hybrids are "VFN resistant." Each letter refers to a specific disease:

- V: Verticillium wilt
- F: Fusarium wilt
- N: nematodes
- TMV: tobacco mosaic virus

GANGBUSTER GRAFTS

GRAFTED TOMATOES are gaining ground with tomato-lovers looking for ways to improve their tomato-growing efforts. You can get grafted plants for determinate and indeterminate varieties, and more options are becoming available all the time. Research shows you can double the number of tomatoes you grow thanks to superstrong plants that resist most soilborne diseases. Buying grafted plants can help you dodge troublesome soilborne diseases like Verticillium wilt and help your plants resist root-knot nematodes. Grafted plants can produce more fruit per plant through improved nutrient uptake. More vigorous root systems make them healthier and more productive.

Grafting fruits for commercial purposes started in Asia in the 1920s when horticulturists first tried the process to prevent Fusarium wilt of melons. Now nearly all tomatoes commercially grown in Korea, Japan, and Australia are grafted. Grafted tomatoes (also cucumbers, eggplants, and peppers) are the result of an old-fashioned propagation method similar to the technique used for grapes, fruit trees, and roses. The top part of one plant, called the scion, is attached to the root system of another plant, called the rootstock. The rootstock for many grafted tomatoes comes from wild, nearly bulletproof tomatoes known for thriving in difficult soil conditions.

There are special instructions for growing grafted tomatoes. You need to plant so the graft union is above the soil line, and you need to remove any side shoots (suckers) that form below the graft. Read and follow the pruning and staking instructions that come with your plants.

GROWING GREAT TOMATOES

As a lifelong Colorado gardener, I've always planted my tomatoes as transplants, either buying plants or starting them indoors from seed. Yet I've heard people speak of wonderfully warm places where a person can plant a tomato seed in the ground and it actually grows into a plant and produces fruit. If you live in a cold, short-season climate like I do, you probably grow from transplants, too. If you're one of those direct sowing folks, all I can say is lucky you.

STARTING FROM SEEDS

Whether you have to (or prefer to) start your tomato seeds indoors, sowing and growing them yourself increases your variety choices. You can order any tomato seeds from catalogs or online retailers, buy them at your local garden center, or swap seeds with fellow growers.

Select the tomato varieties you want to grow, and check the information in the catalog or on the seed packet. Look for the number of days it takes for the seeds to germinate and the number of days it takes from transplanting in the garden until you can start harvesting ripe tomatoes. Plan to start seeds six to eight weeks before the

Starting your own tomatoes from seed will give you a wider selection of varieties to choose from.

Marty Schnicker's
giant tomatoes
weighed 2.3 and
2.43 pounds each.

POTENTIAL PRIZEWINNING TOMATOES

HERE ARE THE TOP 10 tomato recommendations, in three popular categories. They're from tomato-loving gardeners, just like you.

MEDIUM- TO LARGE- FRUITED TOMATOES
- 'Aunt Ruby's German Green'
- 'Big Beef'
- 'Brandywine'
- 'Celebrity'
- 'Juliet'
- 'Kellogg's Breakfast'
- 'Mortgage Lifter'
- 'Orange Russian 117'
- 'Paul Robeson'
- 'Sasha's Altai'

SMALL AND CHERRY TOMATOES
- 'Chocolate Cherry'
- 'Isis Candy'
- 'Sun Gold'
- 'Sun Sugar'
- 'Super Snow White'
- 'Supersweet 100'
- 'Sweet 100'
- 'Sweetie'
- 'Tiny Tim'

MOST FLAVORFUL TOMATOES
- 'Ananas Noire'
- 'Anna Russian'
- 'Black from Tula'
- 'Black Krim'
- 'Black Prince'
- 'Fourth of July'
- 'German Queen'
- 'Lemon Boy'
- 'San Marzano'
- 'Speckled Roman'

average last frost date for your area. Keep in mind the date(s) of the contest(s) you want to enter.

STARTING WITH TRANSPLANTS

Even when you start your tomato garden with transplants, you need to check the number of days to maturity. Make sure there's plenty of time for your crop to be ready in time for the contest.

When your tomatoes first go in the ground, you want to encourage formation of healthy roots instead of ripening existing fruit. So if you're starting with transplants from a nursery or garden center, resist the temptation to buy large plants that are already flowering or fruiting. Instead, look for plants that are dark green, are 6 to 8 inches tall, and have stems about the diameter of a pencil.

WANNA GROW BIG?

Sometimes gardeners just want to stretch the boundaries of tomato growing and go big. Really big. Just imagine a tomato that weighs more than 8 pounds! That was the 8.41-pound 'Big Zac' record-setter grown by Dan MacCoy in Ely, Minnesota, in 2014. No doubt other growers will want a crack at that record.

If you want to try growing a jumbo, giant, or humongous tomato, here are a few expert recommendations to keep in mind:

Start with a cultivar that's meant to grow big. The year I grew my nearly 2-pounder, I planted 'Giant Belgium' seeds, known for growing tomatoes that can weigh 5 pounds. 'Old Colossus' is another known heavyweight, and it's an heirloom, too.

Give plants exactly what they want. Make sure your tomatoes are planted in well-drained soil amended with compost. They'll also need plenty of sun, water, and weekly applications of fertilizer. Allow even more space between plants than usual, and build a heavy-duty trellising system for support.

COMPETING FOR CASH

PERHAPS IT WAS THE LURE OF A LATE-SUMMER ROAD TRIP to Cincinnati, or the possibility of a $2,500 cash prize, that caused Susan Linko and her family to enter their first vegetable contest in 2003. They had just heard about the NatureSweet Homegrown Tomato Challenge the day before and decided to enter some of their favorite tomatoes.

"We won and it was very exciting. It unleashed a monster," Susan says. "Then we really started preparing for the next year's contest and thinking what we'd need to do to repeat the win."

Their attention to detail paid off: they took home the top prize again in 2004. Since those first two contests, they've cashed $15,000 worth of those oversized NatureSweet Homegrown Tomato Challenge checks.

NatureSweet held its first Homegrown Tomato Challenge in 2003 as a simple competition to find the best-tasting home-grown tomatoes. Judges test every tomato for sweetness using a refractometer that measures the approximate amount of a tomato's total sugars. The measurement of sweetness is calculated in Brix units, and the tomatoes with the highest Brix scores are taste-tested by celebrity judges before the NatureSweet staff combines the scores and selects the winners.

Cultivar selection and crop maturity are two key factors that can affect a tomato's Brix level. Environmental factors — moisture, fertility, sunlight, and temperature — also influence Brix levels.

The Linkos credit a base of rich garden soil for their winning ways. The family lives and gardens on a former dairy farm in Harrison, Ohio. Susan, her husband, Pete, and their four kids all contribute to the family's gardening success, planting about 100 tomatoes in their 5,000-square-foot vegetable bed. They also grow green beans, carrots, radishes, lettuce, asparagus, and a horseradish plant that's more than 110 years old.

They enrich the soil every year with homemade compost that includes manure from their horses and something Susan believes is their secret ingredient: Starbuck's coffee grounds. Pete built a motorized composter that churns out mounds of their priceless compost.

The tomato-growing process starts each fall when Pete sends in soil samples for testing. He makes any needed adjustments over the winter so the garden is ready to plant in spring.

"We amend the soil and grow a cover crop of winter rye that we turn over in spring," Susan says.

Pete starts hundreds of tomato plants each year. Many are for their garden, and the rest he gives away to family and friends. "At first I was telling him not to let other people know about the contest," Susan confesses. "But now we invite the competition. It's just so much fun to be there with our family and friends. It's really fun when someone we know wins."

The Linkos plant their tomato crop after Mother's Day in their Zone 6 garden, spacing plants 6 feet apart so they'll grow tall and wide. They irrigate the plants until the tomatoes set fruit and then water only if plants start to wilt. Another secret to their tomato success is watering with harvested rainwater only, never with chlorinated water.

Pete may pick off some of the tomatoes to allow the sugar to go to fewer fruit. "But," Susan says, "we don't mess with the plants a whole lot once they're in."

The two varieties that have been most successful for them are 'Cherokee Purple' in the large category and 'Sun Gold' in the small. Before a contest they'll test a few tomatoes with a refractometer, just like the NatureSweet judges. "We'll check a few tomatoes from each plant to see which are Brixing the highest and then guess which plant to pick from, but that's not always the best tomato," Susan says. "One year we had a 'Sun Gold' Brixing at 14 or 15 and it was a runner-up. The judges voted it too sweet!"

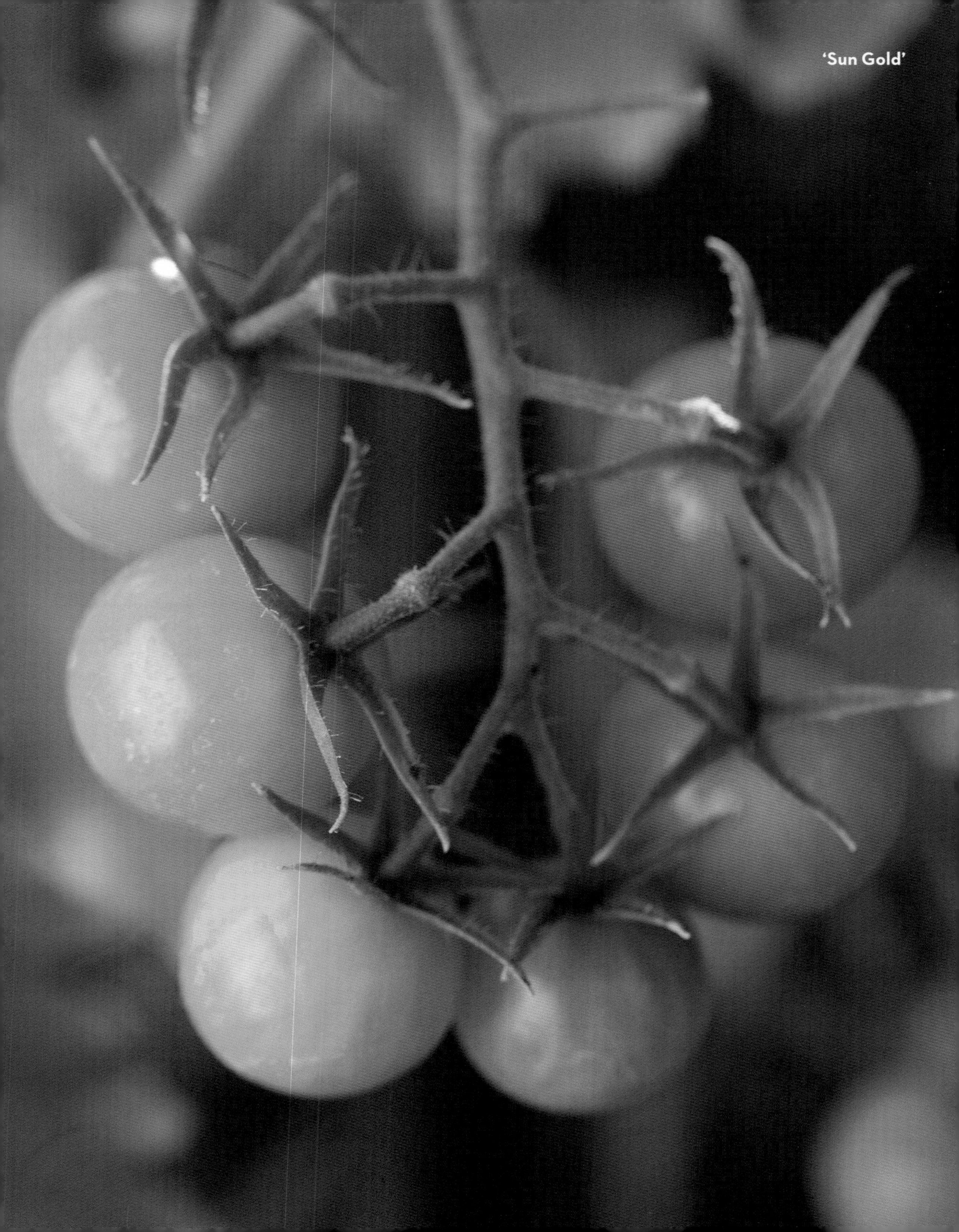

'Sun Gold'

Check plants for monster blooms. These fused flowers are the result of two or more blossoms growing together into one big flower, which will grow multiple conjoined fruits. The resulting bumpy and unattractive fruits are beautiful in a jumbo-tomato, prizewinning way. If there aren't any mega-blooms, thin blossoms to leave just a few.

Help the bees and pollinate the flowers yourself. Use another tomato blossom, a small brush, or your finger to spread pollen among the blooms.

Limit the number of tomatoes. Starting in midsummer, remove all the fruit except for the biggest one on each plant to direct the plant's energy to growing it even bigger.

Prune the plant. Some experts prune to a single vine; others leave a stem plus a secondary branch. Most remove foliage from the bottom 12 inches of the stem to prevent foliar disease. (Spores of soilborne diseases can splash onto low-growing leaves in a heavy rain.) Another pruning method is to cut the top off the vines of tall, indeterminate varieties when they reach about 7 feet.

Support tomatoes so they don't break from the vine. Use lengths of old nylon stockings, old socks, or other similar stretchy material. Creative gardeners have also used old brassieres to cup the fruit for support.

Pick tomatoes before they ripen completely. This keeps them from losing weight while still on the vine.

PLANTING TOMATOES

To grow the tastiest tomatoes, plants need about 8 hours of sun each day. They also grow best in a well-drained, rich loamy soil. To give plants a great start, amend the soil with organic matter and a balanced fertilizer before planting.

Tomatoes benefit from being staked for support.

Before planting in the garden or containers, move tomato plants outdoors and gradually give them a few hours of sun each day to get them acclimated to the outdoors. If nighttime temperatures are chilly, move the plants into a shed, a garage, or the house at night. An alternative is to plant early and use water-filled plant protectors that collect the sun's heat, help warm the soil, and provide warmth at night. Even if you don't plant early, you can use a temporary cover to minimize transplant shock. (See Acclimate before Planting, page 40.)

When the danger of frost has passed and nighttime temperatures reach a reliable 50 to 55°F, plant the tomatoes. If possible, do this late in the afternoon or on a cloudy day to reduce transplant shock. Dig a small planting hole, remove some of the lower leaves from the tomato plant, and place each seedling deeper than it was growing in its pot to encourage growth of more roots.

Plant a minimum of 2 feet apart to give tomatoes plenty of room to grow. Build up the soil to create a small water basin around each plant to collect water and direct it to the roots. Water in with a diluted liquid (or water-soluble) plant food.

Tomato vines will sprawl along the ground unless staked or grown with a tomato cage or trellis. Staking prevents damage to the vines and keeps the fruit off the ground. Plant supports reduce problems with diseases and rotting fruit, plus they put ripe tomatoes in easy reach for harvest. You can make your own heavy-duty tomato cages using concrete-reinforcing wire mesh. Cut a length 6 to 7 feet long and form mesh into round cages. Use 2- to 4-foot lengths of concrete reinforcing rods (rebar) to anchor cages firmly into the ground. In addition to keeping the plants upright in windy weather, the cages make it easier to protect plants from wind by wrapping with plastic sheeting or to cover with insulating blankets and old sheets when cold weather threatens.

MAINTAINING THE TOMATO BED

Every gardener has ideas for what works best for growing high-quality tomatoes. In general,

When nighttime temperatures remain high, tomato plants sometimes lose their flowers, which means you'll have fewer tomatoes.

tomatoes thrive with the same care you give other vegetables, but there are some exceptions. Check plants regularly for signs of insect pests or plant diseases.

Mulch around the plant with an organic mulch such as thin layers of dry, untreated grass clippings or chopped leaves to conserve water, control weeds, and regulate soil temperature. The mulch shouldn't touch the plant stem. Add mulch right after planting, as this helps to prevent disease spores from splashing onto leaves from the soil.

Keep tomato beds free of weeds; take care not to damage roots when weeding. Check soil moisture regularly, and don't let plants dry out. When rainfall is lacking, water deeply; ideally water should penetrate 8 to 10 inches into the soil. Water at the roots of the plant, and avoid splashing water on the leaves.

While plants are growing, some experts recommend pruning to remove all but two growing stems from each plant. The goal is to help plants

Growing in raised beds with red plastic helps warm the soil for this heat-loving plant.

grow vertically and prevent plant disease by allowing for better air circulation. Some growers advise removing leaves from the lower foot of tomato stems as another way to prevent plant disease. Another pruning method is to remove suckers (the branches that grow in the joints of the stems between the leaf and main stalk) to direct energy to growing fewer, but larger fruit. Use your fingers to pinch suckers off while still small.

Use a balanced fertilizer to side-dress tomato plants while flowering and when the fruits are set and begin to grow. Continue to make fertilizer applications every two to four weeks. Keep fertilizing from midsummer to late summer to help plants resist the tomato disease called early blight and to improve the tomato yield. Discontinue fertilizing in mid-August so vine growth will slow and to promote ripening of fruit.

HARVESTING TOMATOES

When tomatoes have reached their mature color and size, use pruners to carefully clip them from their vines. Check for fruit that's slightly soft to the touch and in peak condition for slicing.

Harvest as close to the contest as you can. If necessary, store tomatoes in a cool basement, but don't refrigerate. When tomatoes are refrigerated, their texture turns grainy and they tend to lose their flavor.

PREVENTING TOMATO PROBLEMS

The best way to prevent insect and disease damage to your tomatoes is to cultivate good gardening practices. Refrain from overwatering or underwatering. Keep the tomato bed weed-free, and fertilize on schedule. Then, be observant. Watch for potential problems as tomatoes are growing, and take action as needed.

Weather plays a big part in how well your garden grows. Spring weather can be perfect for planting one day, and then a cold front blows through the next. Cool weather during blossom time may make tomato plants drop their flowers or cause malformed fruit. But cool temperatures aren't the only weather-related worry. If morning temperatures quickly rise above 90°F, blossoms may drop or refuse to develop into tomatoes. Tomatoes are also sensitive to wind, drenching rains, and hailstorms. You can't do much about the weather, but you can work to safeguard plants by using water-filled plant protectors, adding a layer of row cover or shade cloth, or building heavy-duty hail guards.

Poor maintenance practices, insects, or diseases can cause other problems in the tomato patch. Appearance is one of the most important aspects of judging tomatoes in a competition. Little nibbles from the plant's foliage aren't as serious as spots on the fruit. However, poor quality foliage while plants are growing can affect the quality of the fruit. Lack of the right nutrients, plant diseases, and insect pests can make for a frustrating tomato-growing experience. Here are the most common tomato troubles and how to protect your crop:

Tomato hornworms are large green caterpillars that sport white markings and a horn on their hind ends. Hornworms can strip a plant of its leaves in just one day, and they can also eat your tomatoes. Be vigilant; they're hard to spot because they're the same color as the leaves, so look for large portions of leaves suddenly disappearing. If you spot these pests, pick them off by hand and dispose of them in a bucket of soapy water or a paper bag headed for the trash.

Psyllids are tiny insects that like to feed on tomato plants. They cause leaves to turn yellow and curl. Severe infestations can cause plants to stop growing and producing fruit. Look for small insects on the underside of leaves; use insecticidal soap to control these pests.

'Lemon Boy'

'Caiman'

'Yellow Cherry'

CHECKLIST FOR BLUE RIBBON TOMATOES

REVIEW THE RULES for the number of tomatoes required for the class you're entering. Select tomatoes that are uniform in color, shape, and size; they should have a shiny and smooth skin and a pleasant tomato aroma. If the calyx is left on, make sure it's fresh and green. The interior should be bright and meaty with no green around the seeds. However for green (under-ripe) tomato contests, select "mature green" specimens that have a slight pinkish tinge.

PICK

- ☐ Well-matched, uniform tomatoes
- ☐ Ripe, firm, ready to slice
- ☐ Bright color and nicely rounded shape
- ☐ Average to better-than-average size for type
- ☐ Unblemished skin

PASS

- ☐ Immature or overmature fruit
- ☐ Soft spots, cracks, or blemishes
- ☐ Significant size difference

PRESENT

- ☐ Handle carefully to prevent bruising
- ☐ Check rules for showing with or without stems
- ☐ Gently remove soil with a moist cloth

Root-knot nematodes are microscopic soil pests that affect plant roots and stunt growth. Choose tomatoes that are resistant to nematodes (they'll have an *N* after the name, as in VFN). Planting marigolds nearby will discourage these pests.

Blossom-end rot causes a tan or dark, soggy spot on the bottom, ruining tomatoes (and peppers and eggplants, too). It's not a disease but the result of low calcium levels in the soil and inconsistent soil moisture. Prevent blossom-end rot by making sure the soil stays evenly moist to help with uptake of calcium, especially during dry weather. Mulch to help regulate soil moisture and temperature. Test soil pH; tomatoes grow best when pH is around 6.5.

Catfacing results from pollination problems during cold weather. Fruit becomes malformed, winning prizes only in an ugly tomato contest. When selecting varieties that grow larger fruit, choose those known to set fruit in cool temperatures.

Cracks in tomatoes appear as circles at the stem end of the tomato or as cracks that form along the side beginning at the stem. Rapid growth because of wet weather followed by dry weather causes this kind of cracking. Use a soaker hose and mulch to keep the soil evenly moist.

Sunscald is like a tomato sunburn that leaves perfect tomatoes with blotchy yellow skin. Protect fruit from intense sunlight by keeping leaves healthy, and use shade cloth to protect the fruit as it ripens.

Early blight is a disease caused by a fungus; look for brown, circular spots on older leaves before they yellow and die. The disease starts with the lower leaves and slowly progresses up the plant. To prevent early blight,

rotate the tomato bed every year and give tomatoes plenty of planting space to allow air to circulate. Create a strong trellising system to keep tomatoes off the ground, water at soil level, and avoid splashing water on tomato plant leaves.

Late blight is also caused by a fungus, but one that typically infects plants in the middle or late part of summer when the weather is cool and moist. Look for irregularly shaped watery spots on the younger leaves growing on the upper part of the plant. The spots grow larger and cause leaves to shrivel and die. Space tomatoes as far apart as practical, and irrigate plants at soil level. Remove diseased plants from the garden immediately.

Verticillium wilt and **Fusarium wilt** are soil-borne fungal diseases that cause problems in the plant's vascular tissues, leading to plant decline and small, malformed fruit. Plants start to wilt in the middle of the day, even when the soil is moist. Eventually the stems turn brown, the roots may rot, and the plants will produce small, malformed fruit or die. Dispose of any diseased plant parts in the trash, not the compost pile, as there is no effective treatment for these wilt diseases. Your best bet is prevention. When purchasing tomato plants or seeds, buy those that are resistant. They'll be labeled with a *V* and an *F* after the name, as in VFN. Avoid planting tomatoes in the same location every year.

Yellowing leaves can be caused by a number of different maladies, from late blight to various viruses.

SAVING TOMATO SEEDS

IF YOU'VE GROWN A WINNING CROP of open-pollinated or heirloom tomatoes, you might want to save the seeds to grow and enter in future contests. Open-pollinated tomatoes are non-hybrid varieties; they result from natural pollination by insects or wind. Seeds saved from open-pollinated plants will grow the same plant as its parent plant, year after year. (Seeds from hybrids will not produce plants identical to the parent plant.) Heirloom varieties of tomatoes and other vegetables are open-pollinated, which is what allows them to be handed down from generation to generation. Here's how to save seeds from your winning heirloom tomatoes.

Scoop the seeds. Start with one of the best ripe tomatoes from your best plant. Slice the tomato in half across the middle (its "equator"). Use a spoon to scoop out the seeds with the gelatinous goo; place in a clean container. Add enough water to cover seeds. Cover the container with a piece of plastic wrap; poke a small hole in the plastic with a knife or toothpick to allow for air flow. Place the container in a warm location to ferment for several days.

Ferment. Once a day, stir the seed-and-water mixture and then replace the plastic wrap. Watch to see when the top of the liquid looks "scummy," which shows that the fermentation process has separated the goo from the seeds.

Skim and rinse. Remove and discard the scummy surface material. Pour the tomato seeds into a sieve; rinse thoroughly with water. Let drain to remove as much water as possible.

Dry and store. Line a saucer with a piece of waxed paper or a large drip coffee filter. Spread seeds into a single layer on top of the paper. Let the seeds dry for a week or more; stir daily during drying to make sure seeds dry evenly. Seeds are dry when they move quickly and easily across the paper without sticking together.

Store seeds in paper packets or envelopes; label with name of tomato or description. Keep cool and dry until it's time to plant.

★ ACKNOWLEDGMENTS ★

I'VE ALWAYS SAID gardeners are some of the nicest people. After writing this book, I can add librarians to that saying.

I've never appreciated the Internet more than the day I was able to email a request to the Royal Horticultural Society's Lindley Library in London and receive a reply the next day. Carol Westaway, a member of the Enquiries Team, searched the library's vast holdings for books and articles on the history and origins of horticultural exhibitions. She also sent the invaluable link to the Biodiversity Heritage Library, with its massive collection of digitized nineteenth-century gardening books and journals.

Mary Louise Reynnells, a librarian with the USDA's Rural Information Center at the National Agricultural Library in Beltsville, Maryland, was especially helpful on more than one occasion with historical research.

John McKinnie lives in St. Ives in Cambridgeshire, England, and although he isn't a research librarian, he certainly could be. As a blogger at allotmentheaven.blogspot.co.uk, he graciously perused old newspapers on a local library's microfilm to find articles written in the late 1800s about the St. Ives Flower and Produce Show.

I'd also like to thank all the nameless library assistants who searched ancient stacks to find 100-year-old books I requested through Denver Public Library's interlibrary loan system. With every antiquated volume I ordered, I pictured someone trudging down long flights of stairs into a dark basement corner to dust off tomes that hadn't been checked out in decades.

Of course, many other nice folks helped me along the way. Ronda Magnusson, head of vegetable competitions at the Iowa State Fair, narrowed the search to find prizewinning gardeners. Thanks to her, I had the chance to chat with Don Francois, Chuck and Ginger Werner, Marty Schnicker, and Iowa County Extension Director Joe Yedlik. Thanks to Joe, I connected with Jacy McAlexander, an inspiring young competitor.

My gardener's appreciation goes to Dr. Paul Bosland, Dr. Stephen Brown, Amy Goldman Fowler, Bruce Frasier, Jere Gettle, Gary Grande, Chris Gunter, Susan Linko, Bryan Stuart, and Robert Thom for being so generous with their time and expertise.

Thanks to everyone at Storey Publishing, especially Carleen Madigan, for the opportunity to turn my glimmer of an idea into such an enjoyable and rewarding project.

★ RESOURCES ★

IF THIS BOOK PIQUED YOUR INTEREST in agricultural history, vegetable contests, or giant specimen–growing for the fair, you might enjoy scanning through some of these resources.

HISTORICAL TEXTS

All-America Selections
http://all-americaselections.org
Includes all the organization's vegetable winners, from the 1930s to present day

Applewood Books
www.applewoodbooks.com
Reprints of old books, like the classic *The Field and Garden Vegetables of America* by Fearing Burr, Jr. (1865)

**Biodiversity
Heritage Library**
www.biodiversitylibrary.org
Here you can find the texts for many antiquated gardening books.

**National Agricultural Library
The United States Department of Agriculture (USDA)**
http://ric.nal.usda.gov
An exceptional collection of resources on our nation's agricultural history and more

Open Library
https://openlibrary.org
A nonprofit organization that provides an Internet archive and digital library

Rand, McNally & Company
A Week at the Fair.
Rand, McNally & Company, 1893.
A complete guide to the 1893 World's Columbian Exposition held in Chicago; an in-depth look at all the buildings, exhibits, and fascinating features. The entire text is found online using the title in a keyword search.

VEGETABLE CONTESTS

The Bonnie Plants Cabbage Program
334-738-3104
http://bonniecabbageprogram.com
A cabbage contest for third-grade children

International Association of Fairs & Expositions
800-516-0313, www.fairsandexpos.com
A calendar of U.S. fairs and other events

NatureSweet Tomatoes
800-315-8209, http://naturesweet.com
Call or contact NatureSweet for details about the NatureSweet Homegrown Tomato Challenge.

Wallace & Gromit
Wallace & Gromit: The Curse of the Were-Rabbit, directed by Steve Box and Nick Park (2005; Dreamworks Animated, 2006), DVD.
An Academy Award–winning clay animated horror-film spoof. The movie takes a light-hearted look at the wacky world of competitive giant vegetable gardening in Great Britain.

HOW-TO-GROW RESOURCES

LOCAL RESOURCES

**Cooperative Extension System
National Institute of Food and Agriculture, USDA**
800-333-4636
www.nifa.usda.gov/Extension
Who wouldn't take advantage of free, research-based information about growing a great garden? Your county's Cooperative Extension Service can provide specific gardening advice for your climate and hardiness zone, help you find a lab for soil testing, give you accurate seasonal planting information, suggest ways to stymie insect pests, help diagnose plant diseases, and much more. Master Gardeners, garden clubs, and well-staffed local garden centers also may be able to provide good local advice.

The USDA's Cooperative State Research, Education, and Extension Service (CSREES) provides an easy way to find your nearest Cooperative Extension office with an interactive map.

The National Gardening Association
802-863-5251, www.garden.org
A wealth of free resources on gardening basics

GROWING GIANT VEGETABLES

Alaska State Fair
907-745-4827; http://alaskastatefair.org
Dates and details of the annual Giant Cabbage Weigh-Off

The Great Pumpkin Commonwealth
http://greatpumpkincommonwealth.com
All the weigh-off locations and many resources for giant pumpkin competitors

Rocky Mountain Giant Vegetable Growers Club (RMGVG)
www.coloradopumpkins.com
A network of growers across the country (and globe) who share their tips and tricks for growing big

✶ BIBLIOGRAPHY ✶

ONLINE ARTICLES AND BOOKS

Amherst, Alicia. *A History of Gardening in England.* London: B. Quaritch, 1895. www.biodiversitylibrary.org/item/72755.

Brooks, Derek. "Getting Started on the Show Bench." http://garden-friends.co.uk/thread/163/started-on-show-bench.

Clews, Colin. "Trench warfare: cut-throat competition at local leek shows," Views from the Clewsdesk (blog), October 8, 2010. www.clewsdesk.com/trench-warfare-cut-throat-competition-at-local-leek-shows, accessed July 9, 2012.

European Giant Vegetable Growers Association
http://egvga.eu
accessed July 7, 2012.

Georgia State Fair
http://georgiastatefair.org
Fair competition exhibitor books.

Harrison, H. C. "Exhibiting and Judging Vegetables." A3306. University of Wisconsin-Extension, n.d. http://learningstore.uwex.edu/assets/pdfs/A3306.PDF.

Holmes, George K. *List of Agricultural Fairs and Exhibitions in the United States.* Bureau of Statistics, Bulletin 102. Washington: Government Printing Office, 1913. www.biodiversitylibrary.org/item/83301.

Iowa State Fair
www.iowastatefair.org
Fair competition exhibitor books.

Jones, Joy, Beverly Hobbs, N. S. Mansour. "Oregon 4-H Horticulture Contest Guide, rev. ed." Oregon State University Extension Service, 2007. http://extension.oregonstate.edu/catalog/4h/4-h2334.pdf.

Laning, J. F. *How to Manage Agricultural Fairs, Industrial Institutes, and Similar Exhibitions: A Complete Guide for Directors, Secretaries and Officers.* New London, OH: The Fair Printing Company, 1881. www.biodiversitylibrary.org/item/80149.

McKinnie, John. "History of Allotments," Allotment Heaven (blog), http://allotmentheaven.blogspot.co.uk/2009/10/history-of-allotments.html. Email correspondence, July 11, 2012.

Minnesota State Fair
www.mnstatefair.org
Fair competition exhibitor books.

Growing for Show Advice
National Vegetable Society
www.nvsuk.org.uk/growing_for_show.html
Accessed July 10, 2012.

Elkanah Watson Papers, 1773–1884. Manuscripts and Special Collections, New York State Library. www.nysl.nysed.gov/msscfa/sc13294.htm.

Paris, H. S., and J. Janick. "What the Roman Emperor Tiberius Grew in His Greenhouses." Proceedings of the IXth EUCARPIA meeting on genetics and breed of Cucurbitaceae, Avignon (France), 2008. www.hort.purdue.edu/newcrop/2_13_Janick.pdf.

Vegetable Show Planning Guide
Texas A&M University
http://aggie-horticulture.tamu.edu/vegetable/guides/vegetable-show-planning-guide Compiled by Roland Roberts, Tom Longbrake, Sam Cotner, and John Larson. Accessed July, 9 2012.

4-H History: Formation of the 4-H Movement
Virginia Cooperative Extension
http://ext.vt.edu.

Williamson, William. *The Horticultural Exhibitors' Handbook.* Revised by Malcom Dunn. William Blackwood and Sons, 1892. www.biodiversitylibrary.org/item/115170.

Winslow, R. M. *Exhibiting Fruit and Vegetables.* Bulletin 48. W. H. Cullin, 1913. www.biodiversitylibrary.org/item/68671.

BOOKS

Bailey, L. H., ed. *Cyclopedia of American Agriculture: A Popular Survey of Agricultural Conditions Practices and Ideals in the United States and Canada.* Vol. IV: Farm and Community. Macmillan, 1910.

Beattie, W. R. *Cucumber Growing.* U.S. Department of Agriculture, Farmers' Bulletin No. 1563. Government Printing Office, 1928.

Beckett, Edwin. *Vegetables for Exhibition and Home Consumption.* Simpkin, Marshall, et al, 1899.

Bloch-Dano, Evelyne. *Vegetables: A Biography.* Translated by Teresa Lavender Fagan. University of Chicago Press, 2012.

Botkin, B. A. *The American People: In their Stories, Legends, Tall Tales, Traditions, Ballads and Songs.* Pilot Press, 1946.

Corbett, L. C. *Cucumbers.* U.S. Department of Agriculture, Farmers' Bulletin No. 254. Government Printing Office, 1906.

Cowan, C. Wesley, and Patty Jo Watson, eds. *The Origins of Agriculture: An International Perspective, rev. ed.* University of Alabama Press, 2006.

Dean, Alexander. *Vegetable Culture, a Primer for Amateurs, Cottagers, and Allotment-Holders.* London: Macmillan, 1896.

Dewitt, Dave, and Paul W. Bosland. *The Complete Chile Pepper Book: A Gardener's Guide to Choosing, Growing, Preserving, and Cooking.* Timber Press, 2009.

English Vegetable Garden, The. London: The "Country Life" Library, 1909.

Fletcher, Harold R. *The Story of the Royal Horticultural Society 1804-1968.* Oxford University Press, 1969.

Gettle, Jere, and Emilee Gettle. *The Heirloom Life Gardener: The Baker Creek Way of Growing Your Own Food Easily and Naturally.* Hyperion, 2011.

Goldman, Amy. *The Compleat Squash: A Passionate Grower's Guide to Pumpkins, Squashes, and Gourds.* Artisan, 2004.

Gregory, James J. H. *Squashes: How to Grow Them.* Orange Judd & Co., 1867.

Harlan, Jack R. *Crops and Man,* 2nd ed. American Society of Agronomy, Crop Science Society of America, 1992.

Herbst, Sharon Tyler, and Ron Herbst. *The New Food Lover's Companion,* 5th ed. Barron's Educational Series, 2013.

Hoyles, Martin. *The Story of Gardening.* Journeyman Press, 1991.

Kingsbury, Noel. *Hybrid: The History & Science of Plant Breeding.* University of Chicago Press, 2009.

Lavery, Bernard. *How to Grow Giant Vegetables.* HarperCollins, 1995.

Laws, Bill. *Spade, Skirret and Parsnip: The Curious History of Vegetables.* Sutton Publishing, 2004.

Leapman, Michael. *The Biggest Beetroot in the World: Giant Vegetables and the People Who Grow Them.* Aurum Press, 2008.

McPhail, James. *A Treatise on the Culture of the Cucumber,* 2nd ed. London, 1795.

Morrish, R. W. *A History of Fairs.* Books and Bulletins, #4. New York: International Association of Fairs and Expositions, 1929.

Neely, Wayne Caldwell. *The Agricultural Fair.* New York: Columbia University Press, 1935.

Nelson, Derek. *The American State Fair.* MBI Publishing, 1999.

Opperman, Chris. *Allotment Folk.* New Holland Publishers, 2004.

Rupp, Rebecca. *How Carrots Won the Trojan War: Curious (but True) Stories of Common Vegetables.* Storey Publishing, 2011.

Scott, Aurelia C. *Otherwise Normal People: Inside the Thorny World of Competitive Rose Gardening.* Algonquin Books. 2007.

Smith, Andrew F. *The Tomato in America: Early History, Culture, and Cookery.* University of South Carolina Press, 1994.

Warren, Susan. *Backyard Giants: The Passionate, Heartbreaking, and Glorious Quest to Grow the Biggest Pumpkin Ever.* Bloomsbury, 2007.

Watkins, Thomas. *The Art of Promoting the Growth of the Cucumber and Melon.* London: Harding, 1824.

Weaver, William Woys. *Heirloom Vegetable Gardening: A Master Gardener's Guide to Planting, Growing, Seed Saving, and Cultural History.* Henry Holt and Co., 1997.

———. *100 Vegetables and Where They Came From.* Algonquin Books, 2000.

Whitehead, William A. *Contributions to the Early History of Perth Amboy and Adjoining Country.* New York: D. Appleton, 1856.

Wulf, Andrea. *Founding Gardeners: The Revolutionary Generation, Nature, and the Shaping of the American Nation.* Vintage Books, 2012.

BIBLIOGRAPHY

★ INDEX ★

Page numbers in *italic* indicate photos or illustrations; numbers in **bold** indicate charts.

INTERIOR PHOTOGRAPHY BY

© Ryan Donnell, i, ii (all except carrots & Ferris wheel), v, vii (except man with carrots), viii (top right & bottom left), 2–4, 8, 13, 14 (all except left, 3rd from bottom), 16, 18, 21–23, 25–36, 38, 41, 42, 43 (left), 44, 46, 49–52, 53 (top right), 55–57, 59–64, 72, 78, 81, 83–86, 89, 94, 97–104, 106, 108, 111, 112, 114–116, 120–122, 125–127, 129, 131, 132, 134, 136, 139, 140, 142, 145–153, 156, 157 (right), 159–161, 162 (bottom), 163–166, 170, 172–175, 178, 180, 181, 183–187, 190, 193, 196, 201 (left), 203

ADDITIONAL PHOTOGRAPHY BY:

© Anchorage Daily News/Marc Lester/Getty Images, 91 (bottom right); © Arco Images GmbH/Alamy, 87 (top); © Baker Creek Heirloom Seeds/www.rareseeds.com, 24, 118, 119, 176; © Bonnie Plants, 93; © www.bridgemanimages.com, 10; Carolyn Eckert, ii (Ferris wheel), viii (top left & bottom right), 17, 43 (right), 162 (top); © Clinton Francois, ii (carrots), vii (man with carrots); © Daisy Huang, 82; © Dave Bevan/Alamy, 71; © David Cavagnaro, 70, 87 (bottom); © dionisvero/iStockphoto.com, 73; © Courtesy of Dixondale Farms, 128; © Don Francois, 14 (left, 3rd from bottom), 53 (all except top right); © Earl McAlexander, 74, 75; © GAP Photos/BBC Magazines Ltd., 67; © GAP Photos/Chris Burrows, 107; Courtesy of Harrogate Flower Shows, 135; © ImageBROKER/Alamy, 167; © Jacky Hobbs.com, 105; © Jodi Torpey, 154; © John Pendleton, 7, 77, 90, 91 (left & top right), 92, 157 (left), 158, 168, 179, 206; © Kevin Britland/Alamy, 76; © Mar Photographics/Alamy, 182; © merlinpf/iStockphoto.com, 130; © Noèmi Hauser/Getty Images, 66; © Petro Perutskyi/Alamy, 69; © Philary/iStockphoto.com, 133; © Rosalind Creasy, 188, 189; © Shoe Heel Factory, 195, 201 (right), 204; © Stephen L. Garrett, 9, 40, 199, 200, 205

OTHER STOREY BOOKS
YOU WILL ENJOY

EPIC TOMATOES
BY CRAIG LeHOULLIER

Grow your best tomatoes ever! *Epic Tomatoes* explains everything a tomato enthusiast needs to know about growing more than 200 varieties of hybrid and heirloom tomatoes.
256 pages. Paper. ISBN 978-1-61212-208-3.
Hardcover. ISBN 978-1-61212-464-3.

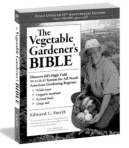

THE VEGETABLE GARDENER'S BIBLE, 2ND EDITION
BY EDWARD C. SMITH

This best-selling classic features Ed Smith's time-tested system for growing an abundance of vegetables, fruits, and herbs using completely organic methods!
352 pages. Paper. ISBN 978-1-60342-475-2.
Hardcover. ISBN 978-1-60342-476-9.

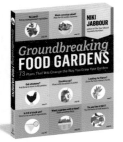

GROUNDBREAKING FOOD GARDENS
BY NIKI JABBOUR

This stellar collection of 73 innovative food garden plans from leading gardeners includes unique themes, innovative layouts, surprise plant combinations, and space-saving ideas. These illustrated designs are sure to ignite your own creativity!
272 pages. Paper. ISBN 978-1-61212-061-4.

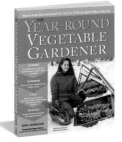

THE YEAR-ROUND VEGETABLE GARDENER
BY NIKI JABBOUR

No matter where you live, you can grow your own food 365 days a year! Learn how to select the best varieties, master succession planting, and make inexpensive protective structures that keep vegetables viable through the winter.
256 pages. Paper. ISBN 978-1-60342-568-1.
Hardcover. ISBN 978-1-60342-992-4.

These and other books from Storey Publishing are available
wherever quality books are sold or by calling 1-800-441-5700.
Visit us at *www.storey.com* or sign up for our newsletter at *www.storey.com/signup*.